Mirror, Mirror

J. O. BALLANCE

This book is dedicated to everyone that listened to me talk for countless hours about this literary endeavor. You will always have a special place in my heart. With your love, encouragement, and support, I kept writing and soared toward my dreams, even though at time I felt like giving up because this path was much more complicated than I anticipated. I hope you enjoy the book. If not, don't tell anyone (Just Kidding). Love you all.

MIRROR, MIRROR

Mirror, Mirror, on the wall, as I sit before you again and wonder if I'd ever love after the breakup with Chase. Three years into a non-marriage with him, I often questioned what compelled me to stay. Like most relationships, it was wonderful in the beginning. The mere thought of him caused my heart to race, and those pheromones flowed like Niagara Falls. I didn't have a checklist for a man, but if I did, Chase would have met all my criteria. He proposed to me our sex life was amazing, and we profoundly wanted the best for each other. So yes, I was caught off guard when he backed out of the marriage. Mirror, I can never retrieve those years with Chase. He was the man who captured my soul but, in the end, pierced my heart with resent-ment. Now, I have no choice but to embrace the emptiness of my space, and I pray another failed relationship is not on the horizon.

Chapter One

Chase was different from most of the guys I met. He was reserved, focused, and unafraid of failure. What impressed me the most was how he viewed failure. He often said, "Failure is a roadmap to success." I connected to those words because I overcame many life and career obstacles. Chase's tenacity became the flame that fueled my aspiration to advance in my career. Not only was he business savvy; but he was also quite attractive.

At thirty years old, he stood at 5'9, with hypnotizing hazel-green eyes, beautiful caramel skin, and a muscular physique that displayed his devotion to fitness with every movement of his body. He wore a close-cropped beard and mustache and often pulled his long-flowing caramel brown and black dreadlocks neatly back in a ponytail. As an entrepreneur, he earned his living as an independent truck driver. He owned a lovely ranch-style home with a pristine yard and was working to purchase additional trucks to expand his business.

In a perfect world, Chase was the perfect man.

~

I met Chase at a BBQ hosted by our mutual friend Jewel in mid-June on a Saturday. While at the BBQ, I noticed the men were outside seated at a card table playing dominoes, so I decided I'd join if given the opportunity. When my time came to play, I sat at the table and introduced myself to the three men, who responded accordingly. When Chase spoke, I immediately noticed his hazel-green eyes. I mused at how rare it was for a Black man to have such gorgeous eyes. Those gorgeous eyes twinkled with a challenge I knew I could meet as one of the men slammed the dominoes onto the table and said, "Let's play!"

I'd always considered myself a good player and wasn't intimidated by their loud trash talk. I strategized when I played the game, and I didn't talk much, but they never stopped, so it was no surprise I won.

"Maybe a little less talking might improve your game," I remarked.

The men chuckled. I rose from the table.

"Who taught you to play?" Chase asked as I started to walk away.

"My older brother."

I returned to the house, poured a glass of pink Moscato wine, fixed a plate of food, and sat at the table with the ladies, ready to brag.

Jewel asked, "Did you win or lose?"

"Girl, you know I wiped the table with their faces," I boasted with a laugh, never noticing Chase standing in the kitchen.

"She's just lucky," Chase said.

"Not lucky," I replied. "Skilled."

"Oh, really?"

"Yes, really. If you need lessons, just call the teacher."

"Okay, Ms. Teacher, can I get your number?"

I paused, gazed at his stunning eyes, and handed over my number.

"By the way, you can call me Michelle."

"Okay, Ms. Teacher," he replied with a laugh. "I'll call you Michelle."

I smiled and returned my attention to the ladies sitting at the table pretending to sip their wine. By the inquisitive look on their faces, I know they were engrossed in the exchange between Chase and me.

~

Throughout the evening, I spotted Chase looking in my direction. Not only did I notice, but Jewel also noticed. "Michelle, I think he's interested in you."

"You think he's interested in me after that dominoes game? Girl, you know how men are. I think I bruised his ego."

"Michelle, I'm telling you he's interested."

"Girl, he's fine. If he asks for a lesson, I'll happily give him one."

With a sly look, Jewel asked. "What kind of lesson, Michelle?"

"Girl, you need to stop. I just met the man. The only lesson he's getting is dominoes."

As I ate my food, I glanced out the kitchen window and noticed Chase looking at me. Shit! Did he notice I was looking at him? I quickly dashed to the bathroom and locked the door.

Why did that have to happen? Why did we have to be looking at each other at the same time? Embarrassed, I regained my composure and returned to the kitchen.

"Michelle, are you okay?" Jewel asked. "You jumped up so quickly."

"Yes, I'm good. It's getting late, and I have a full day tomorrow. You know, going to grocery stores, cleaning, and preparing for the work week. I've got to run. Thanks for the invite."

"Okay, I'll walk you to your car."

"No need. Stay and enjoy your company."

As I turned to leave, Chase approached me.

"Leaving so soon?" he asked.

"Yes, I have a busy day tomorrow."

"On a Sunday?"

"Yes."

"Okay, then. I'll call you later for that private lesson, Michelle."

Eager to keep him interested, I cast him an inviting, encouraging smile.

"Sure, why don't you do that?"

On Tuesday, Chase called and invited me to the Black Girl Art Show hosted by one of his friends at the Pendleton Art Center. I accepted the invitation and met him on Saturday. Unfamiliar with the Black Girl Art Show, I googled it and discovered that this event displayed the artwork of all black female artists. Although I wore an off-the-shoulder knee-length blue jean dress with ankle strap Boho floral wedge sandals, I felt slightly underdressed when Chase showed up wearing blue plaid dress pants with a greenish polo shirt and blue dress shoes.

"Chase, if I'd known this was a dressy occasion, I would have worn a different outfit."

He eyed my honey brown 5'5 frame appreciatively. "Michelle, you look stunning. Don't worry."

"Thanks, Chase, I just feel…"

"Like, I said, you look beautiful. Now let's go inside."

Chase opened the door, and it immediately felt like we stepped into an enchanted land of exotic art. The energy in the room was electrifying and contagious, and the cool sounds of various jazz artists playing on the sound system filled me with eagerness to view the next painting. The paintings were colorfully vivid and evoked serenity. I was impressed by the individuality of the artists as their artwork unapologetically gave me permission to embrace the emotions I felt as I viewed myself in my life's mirror. Chase and I walked around for roughly thirty minutes admiring the paintings before my stomach growled, softly betraying me.

Chase smiled. "Michelle, if you're hungry, we can pause and get some of the hors d'oeuvres."

"Sure, that would be lovely."

As we stood near the counter munching, Chase bumped up against me with a flirtatious look and asked, "When do I get my private lesson, Michelle?"

Jokingly, I replied, "I need to check my schedule, as several men from the BBQ also asked for lessons."

"Oh, so the teacher is in demand?"

"Yes, it appears I am," I said with a laugh.

"Okay, if you say so. Please check your schedule, and let me know?"

"I'll check the minute I get home."

The venue flowed with people, so Chase and I tried to guess their stories. We conjured up tales of hopelessness, freedom of being in the moment, laughter between lovers, and the innocence of not knowing the reality of life. Chase and I remained at the art show for over an hour and then departed. We didn't leave empty-handed, as Chase purchased a one-of-a-kind rainbow-colored painting of a Black woman's eyes for me. I absolutely loved the painting since the eyes are the entryway to the soul and can express sentiments and meaning without the use of words. Our first date was amazing, and I looked forward to our next encounter.

I didn't want to appear too eager to see Chase, so a few days later, I called to invite him over for dinner and a dominoes lesson. He didn't pick up, so I left a message.

Hi Chase, this is Michelle. If you're still interested in a dominoes lesson, you're more than welcome to come over this Friday around 6ish. I'd be happy to give you a lesson with dinner on the side.

While I worked at my desk, my phone buzzed with a text from Chase accepting my invitation. Immediately, my attention shifted from work to planning the dinner.

Now that I had something to look forward to, it seemed as if the work week at Marcell Technologies, Inc. would never end. Could Friday just get here already? I couldn't wait to see Chase's beautiful eyes again. Like the multicolored ocean, his eyes were limitless, hypnotic, and embraced the spirit of a person seeking peace in a majestic place.

When Friday arrived, I rushed home to freshen up and prepare for the evening. I put on a V-neck beige sundress with a tiered skirt that flowed like a beautiful evening wind embroidered with brown flowers and pulled my brown ombre curly shoulder-length hair into a ponytail. Given that I had a fresh pedicure and my toes were painted pink, and to emphasize my right ankle, I decorated it with stackable beaded bracelets in turquoise, beige, and brown. Then I retrieved the dominoes from the kitchen cabinet drawer and placed them on the dining room table. Next, I turned on my Bluetooth speaker and selected a favorite jazz saxophonist, Euge Groove, from my Apple playlist to set the tone for a relaxing evening.

As I prepared dinner, my phone buzzed. It was a text from Chase that read, I'll be there in a few minutes.

I texted back, Okay, see you shortly.

As I returned my attention to preparing the meal, there was a knock on the door.

Chase arrived promptly at six wearing a Nike checkered pink and gray sweatsuit. I was more than impressed by his choice of colors, as men seldom wear pink, but I tried to curb my enthusiasm.

"Hi, Chase. Please come in."

He entered and paused to look around. "Michelle, you have a lovely home. Your retro style is stunning. And I love the bright, colorful painting of tulips above the fireplace. It grabbed my attention straight away."

"Thank you," I said, feeling pleased that he approved of my taste. "Dinner's almost ready. I made spaghetti with a side salad."

"Sounds wonderful. That's one of my favorites."

"Good to hear. Would you like a glass of White Zinfandel or a Stella Artois?"

"Stella, please."

After I handed Chase his beer, we headed to the dining room table for his one-on-one dominoes lesson.

"You're really serious about giving me a lesson?" he asked.

"Yes, I am."

"That's not necessary. Let's just play a couple of games before we eat."

"You sure? I promised you a complete lesson."

"I'm sure. Just being here with you is a win."

We played, and of course, I let him win. For sure, I didn't want to stomp on his ego again.

～

I suggested we enjoy the warm evening breeze by having dinner on my patio under the canopy. While we ate, we noticed two squirrels cheerfully chasing each other across the top of the fence.

Chase paused and said, "If they're not related, then they must be in love."

I inclined my head and looked at him with a smile.

"You know, I'm having a wonderful time, Michelle. And you're an amazing cook."

"Thank you! I'm glad I prepared one of your favorite meals."

"And don't think I didn't notice that you let me win those games."

"I'm afraid I have no idea what you're talking about," I said with a guilty expression.

"Okay, so now you're going to pretend you didn't let me win?"

"Well …"

"That's cool. I had a lot of fun. But I have to say you're quite a skilled player."

"I am. My older brother Aaron loved to gamble, so he taught me how to play cards, dominoes, and dice."

"You must have been close," Chase said.

"Very. He often woke me when he sneaked into the house after curfew to show me all the money he won. That piqued my curiosity, and I wanted to know what he did to get it. When he told me, I asked him to teach me, then we started going out together to play."

"That sounds a little dangerous."

"No, it wasn't like that. We just played with his friends. The more I played, the better I became. What about you?" I asked. "What were you interested in growing up?"

"Having my own business," Chase said. "My dad established a successful landscaping business from home. My siblings and I worked with him. The experience helped me realize at a very young age that I wanted to own a business because it would allow me the freedom to be creative and set my own work schedule. So now I own a small over-the-road trucking company."

He glanced at his watch. "You know, I could sit here and talk with you all night, but it's getting late. I don't want to overstay my welcome. If you're not teaching a dominoes class next weekend, would you like to catch an afternoon movie on Saturday?"

"Sure, that would be fun."

"Okay, then it's a date," Chase said. "Let me help you with the dishes before I leave."

After Chase left, I sat on the loveseat in my den with a glass of my favorite Stella Rosa Moscato wine, turned on the television, and reflected on the evening. It had been a huge success, and it seemed like we had a connection, but was I ready to start dating? I had very little free time as I was involved in the mentoring program at work and focused on advancing my career.

But the more I thought, the more I wondered, What did I have to lose? If the third date revealed red flags, I'd respectfully place him in the friend category. I wasn't worried about what he thought of me, as I was always authentic when I met men. Considering our third date would be at the movies, and the temperature would be in the high 80s, I decided to wear a multicolored tank top, brown wedge sandals, and a pair of pink jeans shorts to show off my toned legs.

Chase called earlier in the week and offered to pick me up. I declined, as we were still getting familiar with each other, and if the date were a bust, I wouldn't have to ride awkwardly with him in his car. So, we agreed to meet at the entrance. I finished getting dressed and drove to the theater. I arrived fifteen minutes before the movie started.

While I walked to the theater, I spotted Chase standing at the entrance wearing khaki shorts, a light blue, short-sleeve shirt, and white sneakers. I looked him up and down as I approached and thought, Damn! He's hot. Chase extended his hand, and I graciously accepted.

As we walked into the theater, he said, "I already bought the tickets. Would you like some popcorn and a drink?"

"Yes, a small popcorn and a bottle of water."

"Okay, why don't you wait here while I get our snacks?"

A few minutes later, Chase returned with two small popcorns and drinks.

"Michelle, I bought tickets for a comedy. I hope that's fine with you."

It really didn't matter what movie he chose; I was just happy to be out of the house on a date with him.

"Yes, that's fine."

As we walked into the movie theater, I noticed Chase bought tickets in the reserved seating. I sat down in the comfortable recliner and stretched out. It was clear Chase had pulled out his gentleman's card today.

"Michelle, are you comfortable?"

"Incredibly so," I said.

As we watched the movie, Chase reached over and placed his hand on my leg, and I placed my hand on top of his hand. We held that position for a few minutes. Feeling his hand on my leg, I couldn't even focus on the movie, and honestly, it was a distant blur in my mind.

Chase leaned over. "Enjoying the movie?"

"Very much," I lied.

Throughout the movie, I wondered why he placed his hand on my leg. Did he assume I'd be comfortable with it? Was that a hint for sex, or was it to make me feel comfortable because he was interested in me? While I was unsure of his reasons, his hand stimulated every nerve in my body, and it felt damn good!

Lost in thought, I didn't even realize the movie was over. Afterward, Chase invited me to join him for a late lunch and drinks.

"Michelle, if you don't have any plans, would you like to join me for lunch at the Cheesecake Factory?" he asked.

Since I had no other plans, I accepted, and we met at the restaurant.

We arrived at the restaurant after the lunch crowd had dispersed. It was rather nice and quiet, and we didn't have to wait for a table. The hostess immediately seated us in a booth and provided two menus. As I perused the menu, I was pleasantly surprised to see meatless burgers since I was health-conscious and tried to eat less meat. When the waitress returned to take our order, I ordered the veggie burger with fries, and Chase ordered the Kobe burger with fries. So far, our Saturday date was amazing and romantic, and I wished I'd let him pick me up.

"You know, Ms. Teacher…. Oh, my bad! I meant Michelle," he said with a laugh. "This may seem somewhat rushed, but I think you and I should start seeing each other more. I realize I don't know you that well, but I'd love the opportunity to learn more about you."

Fully enjoying the atmosphere, I gave in, and my almond-brown eyes gazed into his bewitching hazels. I took a sip of my drink and leaned back in the leather booth.

"Chase," I paused. "I don't know. My work weeks are hectic, and I look forward to the weekends to take it easy and catch up on housework. You need to understand that I can't see you that often. But if you can work with my schedule, I'd love to spend more time with you."

"No worries, Michelle. With my schedule, I'm on the road for one to two weeks each month, so this will work perfectly for us. We just need to plan our dates. What do you think?"

"Okay! Let's give it a try."

We finished our meal, and Chase walked me to my car. When we arrived at my car, he gazed into my eyes, slowly pulled me close, and kissed me on the forehead. What the HELL! A forehead kiss. I just knew he was going to kiss me on the lips!

"Michelle, thanks for making this a lovely Saturday."

"My pleasure. I equally had a great time." I wanted to say, "What's up with the forehead kiss?" But I had to admit the kiss got my panties wet, and I wanted more.

"Until next time, Ms. Teacher," he said with a smile.

"Ha, ha, you got jokes."

We both laughed, said goodbye, and departed.

Chapter Two

Considering our limited time together, we successfully managed our relationship for two years. Chase eventually decided to sell his home and move in with me. When he took a break from the road, our relationship was filled with passionate lovemaking, late-night movies, and home-cooked meals. We certainly didn't want to squander our precious time together entertaining our friends. Our time together ticked like the hands on a clock, so we cherished every passing minute.

On the nights before Chase returned to the road, we lay entwined in bed and made love like there was no tomorrow. I never looked forward to saying goodbye because, as a truck driver, he faced danger on and off the road, and I always feared for his safety. Without fail, before every trip, I always prayed for his safety and showed him just how much I'd miss him. Besides making love, I prepared his meals for the road and helped him pack his truck.

Before Chase's departure, and as we lay in bed, I said, "Chase, I'm really going to miss you."

"Likewise, Babe."

"I know you have to get back to work, but can you possibly stay one more day?"

"Babe, I wish I could, but I've committed to picking up a load in Dallas."

Trying to contain my emotions, I whispered, "I understand."

Chase cupped my face in his hands. "Michelle, from the moment I met you, I knew we'd be together. Unlike most women I've met, you understood and accepted the limitations of our relationship. You encouraged and supported the expansion of my business, and for that, I'd love for you to be my wife."

He reached for the nightstand drawer and pulled out a small velvet box. My heart skipped a beat when he opened it to reveal a gorgeous diamond engagement ring set on a band encrusted with rows of tiny diamonds. The ring sparkled like a constellation.

"Michelle, will you marry me?"

Overwhelmed with emotion, I began to cry. "Chase, my sweetheart, this has always been my dream—to have a husband and children."

"Then this is a dream we'll share," he said.

Without hesitation, I accepted his proposal and dreamed of a beautiful spring wedding.

Everything I hoped to accomplish was now coming to fruition. I'd planned to get married by thirty and start a family a few years later. I had a promising profession as an acquisition specialist when I met Chase. I was twenty-six years old, and now two years later, marriage was imminent. To top it off, Chase's business was thriving, and with less than four months to becoming Mrs. Michelle Olivia Davis-Halston, I was in the finalizing stage of my dream wedding. My happiness glowed like a sun-kissed ocean at dusk. Nothing could shatter that perfect image, or so I thought.

Chase's trucking business began to consume most of his time, and as a rational woman, I understood the intricate details of building a company. I, therefore, continued planning the wedding and updated him on the details, which allowed him to remain focused on his business. As we approached the three-year mark, I hadn't seen Chase in three weeks.

When he finally returned home, he was physically and mentally exhausted. I didn't want to burden him with the wedding plans, considering that he still had to complete his administrative paperwork. This meant tracking the expenses of the truck drivers and following up with the Department of Transportation to confirm all permits and required documents were current, completed, and filed on the trucks. A couple of days later, after Chase completed his paperwork and was resting on the couch watching TV, I approached him to discuss the wedding.

"Babe, if you're up to it, can I talk to you about the wedding plans?"

Something in Chase's eyes shifted like blinds dropping behind a window. My heart sank when I noticed he couldn't quite meet my gaze.

"Michelle, I've been meaning to talk to you about this, but now that you brought it up, I think we should postpone the wedding. The business is just taking up too much of my time."

I felt like I'd been punched in the stomach. From his tone, he might as well have been discussing the weather instead of our wedding.

"What?" I gasped. "Are you serious? Why didn't you tell me before I made all the arrangements? I told you I booked a venue and mailed the invitations. Not to mention

I'm already out of pocket thousands of dollars. You've got to be kidding me!"

Chase sighed tiredly. "No, I'm not kidding, Michelle. I need you to understand that I love you, and our current situation doesn't have to change. But I've got far too much on my plate, and it's essential that I thoroughly understand what I need to run a trucking business. I just need more time to get the business running smoothly."

I shook my head as if to purge his words from my mind. A thousand conflicting emotions roiled in my gut. Was this the same man who proposed to me two months earlier?

"This is unbelievable! You've been focused on this business for over three years, which you were doing even before we met, yet you still don't understand what's required? Seriously? And you still need more time? Then why the hell did you propose? What was the point?"

"Michelle, at the time, I thought ..."

"Thought what? So just like that," I hollered, snapping my fingers, "the wedding's off with no consideration of what I've invested?"

"For now, yes. As I said, it's not a good time. You know, I bought two trucks and hired additional drivers. Basically, if the wheels don't turn, I don't earn." Chase clicked the remote to change the channel on the television.

I blinked at him in astonishment. "Why didn't you ask me for help, Chase? I would have rearranged my schedule, but you never asked. And if you were having second thoughts, you sure as hell should have discussed them with me! You certainly had time to think about it while driving all those miles on the road!"

"Come on, babe, you know you're just as busy." Chase sighed. "That's why we have to plan our schedule just to spend time together. I'm sorry. I meant to bring it up, but it just slipped my mind."

"Oh, it slipped your mind," I spat. "We've been

together for almost three years, and I've supported your ass every step of the way, and now you want me to wait? Wait for how long, another three years?"

"Look, I'm just saying that we need to hit the pause button until the business is efficient and profitable. Then I can come home more often. I just don't want to be on the road for two or three weeks when we're married. I want to be home more often after I get married."

"Chase, you're full of shit!" I cried. "We've managed our relationship with little to no issues with you on the road. Now, all of a sudden, you don't want to get married because you want to be home more often! Obviously, the wedding has been an issue for a while. So really, why now?"

Chase's eyes flashed angrily. "Michelle, I told you, I just need time to focus on the business!"

"First of all, who the hell do you think you're yelling at? You created this mess, not me!"

"Look, Michelle, you know I care about you. I just need more time to sort things out. Can you give me that?"

Sarcastically I said, "You can have all the time that you need. But, tell me this, what the hell do I do about notifying our family and friends?"

"I don't know! Call them, email them, and just let them know we changed our minds. I don't have the energy for this discussion. Let's just table this subject for now, please?"

I slammed my hand on the armrest. "So, let's be clear, Chase. You didn't consider my feelings. You made the sole decision to postpone the wedding despite the arrangements I've already made and the money I've spent. And now, four months until our wedding, you want me to tell everyone we changed our minds? Nah, player. We didn't change our minds. You did!"

"Michelle, you really need to calm down. Weddings

have been canceled or postponed before. I'm sure you can find a way to handle the arrangements."

"Well, aren't you the confident one!" I retorted. "You better damn well hope I can get my money back because you'll be reimbursing me if I don't! As for calming down, not going to happen anytime soon. I think it's time you got back on the road!"

"Michelle, you're making a big mistake asking me to leave. Let's just take a moment and let cooler heads prevail. I don't want to say anything I might regret, or you say something drastic that you might regret."

"Drastic decision!" I snapped, clapping my hands. "That's priceless! You already made a drastic decision by calling off the wedding. So again, I'm not about to cool off. And just to keep it real, I'm sorry I ever accepted your proposal!"

"That's what I'm talking about," Chase said. "You're saying things you don't mean."

"Wrong! You know me, and you know I don't mince words. I meant what I said!"

By Chase's physical reaction, I could tell that a vortex of anger spun in his mind. Suddenly, he slammed the remote on the table and said, "You're blowing this all out of proportion! I'm not asking you to wait forever. I'm just asking you to wait until I get the kinks worked out."

"Chase, I've waited for three years, and you knew I wanted a family. I'm not getting any younger, and I'm not going to wait another three years. You need to understand that I'm completely blindsided by your decision to postpone our wedding. You should have had the decency and respect to spare me the bullshit and simply tell me your feelings have changed!"

"Are you giving me an ultimatum, Michelle? It certainly sounds like it. If that's the case, it won't work for me!"

"No, I'm not giving you an ultimatum. I just don't understand your reasons for calling off the wedding."

"I didn't call off the wedding. I just want to postpone it because I don't want to start our married life with me always on the road. I want the business to run smoothly. Why is that so difficult to understand?"

I shook my head and glared at him in disgust. "Chase, just answer a damned simple question. Do you want to get married?"

"I already told you nothing in our relationship has to change!"

"That's not what I asked. Do you want to get married?"

Chase stood with his arms crossed and the index finger of his partially clenched fist over his upper lip. "Yes, just at a later date, and you're being so inflexible! I'm simply asking for time to get my business in order so we can start our marriage on the right foot. But it looks like you're unwilling to compromise."

I leaped from the couch. "I'm not being flexible? That's all I've done over the last three years. You know what, Chase, you're right. Let's take a break. During this break, I recommend that you find somewhere to live. You're not staying in my house, getting the best of what I have to offer without a commitment, and then deciding you want something different. I'm going to move forward with my life, and I'm not waiting for you!"

Chase looked me coldly in the eye. "Michelle, if I leave, I'm not coming back."

Blinking back tears, I stomped towards the kitchen. My heart ached with every breath. Was this really happening?

"Michelle!" Chase shouted. "Don't turn your back on me. I'm talking to you!"

I continued to the kitchen as though I didn't hear him. As far as I was concerned, there was nothing else to discuss. This had never happened to me, but I've witnessed this scenario in the lives of others, and quite often, the marriage never came to fruition. Realistically, I knew postponement of the wedding was not the end of the world, but there was no way in hell I was going to waste precious time hoping he'd actually marry me.

Chase had the best of both worlds. He had the freedom of the road, the luxury of a comfortable home, and sex whenever and however he wanted it. Of course, he wasn't in a rush to get married. Our relationship was uncomplicated from the beginning and remained that way till the end. I loved Chase and wanted to be his wife. I felt so betrayed and knew if I decided to wait, there would be mistrust and resentment.

So I closed the door to that chapter of my life.

Chapter Three

Now that our relationship was over, I felt insignificant, melancholy, and lonely, with only memories of Chase and a broken proposal. I pondered and debated endlessly what it was about me that seemed to put men off marriage. I had no children, was well-educated, financially independent, enjoyed an excellent career, and I owned a lovely, immaculate home. There was no reason for me, a successful Black woman, to compromise my dreams for a family when all of the pieces of my life's puzzle were in place. I was easygoing and far from demanding, and I knew how to take care of my man.

So, what did I miss?

Three months later, why was I still curled up on the harper-green sectional in my three-bedroom, two and half-bath Craftsman-style home, consoling myself with a box of Kleenex? While the tissues stemmed my tears, they couldn't absorb the pain of my shattered heart. I buried my face in the pillow and curled up in a fetal position for hours, contemplating death. At least, it temporarily silenced the darkness angrily whirling in my mind. The bleeding waterfall of my heart yearned for comfort, for a human touch. I prayed to the Lord to ease my pain. I couldn't go on like this—an empty shell of a woman who only wanted a husband and children.

I recognized that I had to pull myself out of these spiraling emotions, but all I could do was continue mourning the loss of yet more time. More years. More opportunities to build the future I always wanted. It was like the same song replaying on an endless loop. I'd been told that the definition of insanity was a person repeating the same thing expecting a different outcome. But was it insanity to yearn for the comfort of love, a family, and a happy future?

As I sat with my mirror during my dark journey through self-pity, I recalled a time I slept with a man hoping he'd see something special in me. I was more of an introvert, and typically I didn't go out with friends. I enjoyed staying home, relaxing with a good movie, or listening to an audiobook. On the one night that I decided to go out with friends to a nightclub, this happened.

A group of men was sitting at the opposite table. One of them approached and looked me square in the face.

"Hi, would you like to dance?"

"Sure."

"By the way, I'm Deon."

"Nice to meet you, Deon. I'm Michelle."

Before I had time to react, he reached for my hand and led me to the dance floor. I was somewhat hesitant because dancing was not my forte. I was fortunate that the dance floor was crowded and restricted movement. As the thumping music vibrated throughout my body, I began to sway back and forth to the rhythm. I lifted my hands over my head, moved my hips, and forgot about my lack of dancing ability. Deon admired my moves, and we grooved together for two songs.

Afterward, he invited me to join him for a drink. We sat at the bar sipping our drinks, talking, laughing, and for a brief moment, it appeared as though we were two wandering souls who'd found each other.

"Deon, it was a pleasure meeting you this evening. Thanks for the dance and drink."

"Likewise, Michelle. It's been a joy meeting you. Thanks for dancing with me."

Smiling, I said, "I really enjoyed it!"

"Well, if you like, we can take one more twirl around the dance floor before you leave."

"Sure, why not?"

The music shifted from upbeat to a slow groove. I knew I should have declined, but I let Deon lead me back to the dance floor. As we approached, all I heard was the drum-beat of my heart.

Deon pulled me close, wrapped his arms around my waist, and whispered, "Relax. I got you."

I relaxed and let the music become the ocean that swept me to the shore of his arms. Immersed in the hypnotic rhythm, we danced in an unspoken conversation.

When Deon later escorted me to my table, he leaned down and whispered, "This evening doesn't have to end."

I looked into his eyes and found the answer I was seeking. I felt buzzed and more than a little audacious, so I told my friends I was leaving.

As I followed Deon to his house, I thought, Girl, you don't even know this man. What the hell are you doing? I knew his name, but I didn't have his phone number, so I couldn't text my friends his contact details. I should have turned around and gone home, but my need for acceptance was as powerful as the Earth's gravitational pull. I thought we had a connection at the club, so surely, he wouldn't harm me.

My instinct soon proved foolishly naive. I continued to follow him to his place. As soon as we stepped inside, he was all over me, pulling at my clothes while removing his. Immediately, I realized I made an enormous and potentially deadly mistake. It was stupid of me to go to a stranger's place and no surprise that he was treating me like a whore. I offered it easily enough. Now, he was getting what he wanted for free, and there was nothing I could do.

Fearful that he might hurt me if I didn't cooperate, I shifted gears and participated. As he kissed my neck, I whispered that I had to pee. He directed me to the bathroom. Once inside, I locked the door and sat on the toilet. Holding my head in my hands, I started to cry softly. Oh God, what have I done? How do I get out of this predicament?

Then, a knock on the door.

"Hey, you, okay?"

For a moment, I could only stare blankly.

"Yes, I'm fine. I'll be out in a minute."

As I sat there, I thought I just had to pee, but instead, I shit. There was my way out! I'd tell him I just took a shit! There was no way Deon would want me with a nasty asshole. But as soon as I opened the door, he was waiting in the hallway. He grabbed me and started leading me toward the bedroom.

I quickly stopped. "I just took a shit. I'm not feeling well, so I'm going to leave."

"It's just your nerves," he soothed. "No problem, you can take a shower."

In my mind, I screamed, What the HELL! A shower! I knew there was no way Deon would agree to me leaving now! Out of fear, I returned to the bathroom, stripped down, and took a shower. When I pulled back the shower curtain, he was standing in the bathroom with a towel wrapped around his body. I was surprised and more than a little scared.

Nervously, I reached for the towel on the rack, but before I could grab it, he authoritatively stated, "There's no need to dry off."

Dripping wet, I cautiously stepped out of the shower. Deon immediately dropped his towel, and before I could react, he grabbed me and bent me over the sink. He opened the medicine cabinet, retrieved a condom, and effortlessly slipped it on. Before I could process what was happening, he jammed his dick inside me.

Sometimes you wonder how you'd react in a frightening or extreme situation. While my thoughts were running wild, my body refused to respond. I wanted to scream at him to stop, but it would have been pointless. In Deon's hands, I was nothing more than a rag doll to be used how he wanted. He yelled at me to grab onto something, so I reached for the towel rack and held on as tightly as I could, but the damned thing detached from the wall. I knew that if I didn't balance myself, I'd end up getting hurt. I tried to push him back because the pain from his thrusting was intense.

I desperately thought, Please, Lord, let this man finish! I can't take it anymore! I could tell he was about to cum, but out of desperation and the fear that Deon would push my head into the wall, I grabbed onto the toilet and prayed the condom wouldn't break!

At that moment, my thoughts strayed to other women who found themselves in my situation. How many of them have done the same thing? How many of them have put themselves at risk with a man, hoping he'd consider their feelings or just be that special someone they dreamed of finding? More often than not, it was far from the romantic fantasy playing in their minds. Instead of expecting love or some fairy tale magic, they ended up with the opposite or something far worse. I was lucky I didn't get hurt or venture toward worse.

After Deon finished, my legs barely supported me. Everything felt surreal. I glimpsed myself in the mirror but didn't recognize the face staring back at me. He took my hand and led me to the bedroom. Pulling back the sheets, he got in the bed, pulled me next to him, and said, "Close your eyes and go to sleep. I'm not going to hurt you."

After what had just happened in the bathroom, I was frightened and shaking uncontrollably. Deon felt me shaking and pulled me closer. Again, he said, "Close your eyes and go to sleep. I promise I won't do anything else to you."

My imagination kicked off into high gear. Girl, if you fall asleep, you might wake up with this man standing over you with a rope or handcuffs. If you stay awake, then you can at least try and fight.

As I lay there imagining the worse and listening to Deon snore, I struggled to stay awake but somehow dozed off. I woke up to him kissing my shoulder.

"Good morning, Ms. Lady."

Damn, he forgot my name!

"I want to apologize for last night. When you pulled back the shower curtain, I just couldn't control myself. You looked so innocent and sexy. I wanted last night to be memorable, and I failed. I made it all about me. For that, I'm sorry."

In my mind, I thought that it was more about him forgetting what happened in the bathroom!

"So, if you're willing," Deon continued, "I want to pleasure you and give you what I should have last night. I realize women are often degraded for sleeping with a man on the first encounter, but the emanation of self-confidence that flowed from you was refreshing because you knew what you wanted and weren't ashamed to admit it. So please forgive me for my actions and permit me to make love to you."

I looked him in his eyes, pulled his face gently toward me, and kissed him.

"Yes, please make love to me."

Before I left Deon's place, he said, "If you want to meet again, please give me a call."

I looked at him and boldly said, "This morning's sex was amazing, but we both know what this is."

I got in my car and drove home. I never saw my one-night stand again. What had the potential of being a terrible experience, fortunately, turned out to be mind-blowing!

After my melancholy and regrettable trip down memory lane, I gathered the strength to get off the couch and went to the bedroom. I crawled into bed, pulled the covers over my head, and drifted off to sleep with the Mirror.

Mirror, Mirror on the wall, there's more to me beyond my thighs. Blinded by lust, I cannot rise, for what lay beside me was one big lie. I've always been fully conscious of my actions and have done things that birthed sorrow and regret. Now I stand here alone, drowning in the dark abyss of my life's insane reality. Again, please tell me it can't be, that this is not the woman's reflection you see. You've been with me from birth, and you've watched me soar to the heights of success and plunge to the greatest depths of despair.

Mirror, although I was distracted by a lover, I'm now struggling to regain control of my thoughts. In your view, you see me as a strong woman, and you know I'll always do whatever it takes to survive since I can be fearless as a lioness or as gentle as a lamb. Is it possible that I'm damaged, but surely, the damage is reversible? I'm aware I should find confidence in my reflection and never allow negativity to define my future, but at this moment in time, my mirror's image is faceless in the dark. If I can only find the strength to rise, then love will find me.

Chapter Four

The next day, I woke up to a cool March morning. The dull light filtering through the window ushered in a physical and mental chill that sent me burrowing beneath the covers. I hit the snooze button and went back to sleep. When the alarm sounded again, I realized I'd overslept. Shit! I quickly jumped out of bed. There was no time to shower, so I took a quick sponge bath and got dressed.

I hurried to the garage and jumped into my car. I was fortunate that my commute to work was only ten minutes. No matter where I lived, I made it a point to live as close to work as possible to avoid lengthy commuting. When I arrived in the parking garage at work, I realized I couldn't allow my sadness and disappointment to set the tone for the week. After I parked, I prayed and thanked the Creator for my blessings and the gift of another day.

As I rushed toward the office building, I noticed an attractive, tall, well-built man with earthy-brown skin standing near the entrance. He appeared to be looking in my direction, and I wondered if he was looking at me. Girl, don't you dare look at him. Just pretend you're looking at something. For damn sure, I didn't want him to notice my miserable face. Oh, Lord, I have to walk past him.

I nervously pulled myself together and forced my legs to move forward. Legs, please don't stumble, don't fall, don't trip, just move! As I approached, he began to wave. I looked around and noticed only a few people in the area. Surely, he wasn't waving at me. I walked as though I hadn't noticed he was waving.

As I approached the entrance, he was still waving, so I waved and said, "Good morning."

"Excuse me?" he said.

At that moment, I'd have been happy if the ground had opened up and swallowed me. OMG, girl. He wasn't waving at you!

Quickly, I blushed, "I thought you were ..."

I knew he saw my embarrassed expression, so he just nodded his head. Considering I just made a fool of myself, he could have at least said good morning! Of all the people walking in the building, why did I have to assume he was waving at me? As I walked past him, my heart hammered so loudly from the embarrassment that I thought everyone could hear it. Yet throughout the day, I couldn't stop thinking about the attractive man that stood at the entrance of the building.

Why did I wave? I should have just walked into the building and kept my mouth shut! Regardless, a good morning from him would have made my gloomy Monday morning a little brighter. Here I go again, getting all in my head, thinking about a man who doesn't even know who I am and probably doesn't care to find out.

As I prepared to leave work at the end of the day, I prayed I wouldn't run into him as I left the building. Seeing him would ignite my chaotic emotions. I gathered my belongings and practically jogged to the exit. Faintly, I heard the security guard, Mr. Shelton, calling me. I looked at him and noticed my morning man near the security guard station. Oh no, this wasn't good! Girl, don't you dare make eye contact with him! Look away. Pretend you're looking for something in your bag! Do it now before Mr. Shelton notices you. I walked with shaking knees and sweating palms. Mr. Shelton continued calling me. I knew it was rude to ignore him, but I didn't care, so I kept walking.

"Ms. Davis!" Mr. Shelton yelled. "Ms. Davis!"

Damn, he's not going to stop!

I approached the guard station and forced myself not to look at the handsome stranger.

"Hi, Mr. Shelton. What do you need?"

"You wanted me to let you know when my granddaughter would be selling Girl Scout cookies."

"Oh, now I remember!"

"I'll have some next week. Please stop by and pick up a couple of boxes. She'll greatly appreciate the support."

"Of course, I will!"

"Ms. Davis, please forgive my rudeness. Let me introduce you to Everett James. Everett works on the second floor in the Human Resources Department."

"Nice to meet you, Mr. James," I said, feeling embarrassment flush my face yet again.

"Didn't we meet this morning?" Everett asked.

"Ah, well, I thought you were waving, so I…"

He smiled. "No worries. It's all good. You can call me Everett."

I nodded and continued speaking with Mr. Shelton. I noticed Everett wanted to join the conversation but seemed unsure how to politely interrupt. Finally, when there was a break in the conversation, he spoke.

"Ms. Davis, despite what happened this morning, how was your day?"

"It was productive. Please call me Michelle."

"Sounds good. I figured you might have been dwelling on what happened this morning."

I chuckled. "Not at all. I had plenty of work to deal with."

"If you say so," he said with a laugh.

"Ms. Davis, do you plan to attend the Spring Has Sprung event this year?" Mr. Shelton asked.

"I haven't decided yet."

"Well, if you're looking for someone to escort you," he said with a smile. "Everett here is single, and I'm almost certain he'd love to accompany you to the event."

What the hell! Why would he say that? I'm not some desperate woman who needs an old man to fix her up with a date!

Yes, I may have assumed Everett was waving at me, but really? Mr. Shelton was a sweet old man who meant no harm, but he had a knack for saying things at the wrong time. We both just stood there looking at each other. I'm sure Everett was thinking, What makes you think I want to take her to the event?

Everett stood about 6'2. His clothes were neat and tailored, and he smelled good. The only thing unattractive about him was his teeth. How could this handsome man have ugly teeth? The more he talked, the more I stared at his teeth. I knew that was rude, but my eyes had a mind of their own. I was not superficial and normally didn't judge someone by their appearance, but damn! However, during our conversation, I realized that Everett had all the confidence in the world because he continued to talk and smile.

I briefly wondered if I could kiss him. Initially, the answer was a hard, hell-to-the-no. But as I listened to him talk, I noticed his assured demeanor and realized the answer was yes. For some people, their teeth can make or break a deal. For me, that became inconsequential. What attracted me was his self-confidence, swag, and light-heartedness.

"I won't need an escort to the event, Mr. Shelton," I said. "Have a good evening."

As I walked away, Mr. Shelton yelled, "Don't forget! I'll have the cookies next week."

I glanced over my shoulder and gave him a thumbs up. I knew Everett was watching, so I had to appear poised. As my legs once again shook like an out-of-balance washing machine, I thought, Legs, please don't let me down. We're almost at the door!

Afterward, I came to look forward to the end of each workday and left the building as slowly as possible in the hopes of seeing Everett. After I met him, I felt like the unhappiness weighing me down had been lifted, and a spark of joy flowed through my body. Or was it simply that I needed the companionship of a man?

While I wasn't sure, I knew I wanted to explore it. Time passed, and I hadn't seen Everett in over a week. Should I ask Mr. Shelton? If I did, he'd certainly think I was desperate. I decided to let it go.

Two weeks later, as I walked toward the building entrance, I saw Everett in the parking garage with a young woman. From what I could tell, they appeared to be having a pleasant conversation. I thought, No wonder he didn't offer to escort me to the event. He is in a relationship. I slowed my pace and watched them walk toward the entrance.

Everett paused to open the door for the young woman. What a gentleman! I mentally shook my head.

Michelle, here you go again, letting your emotions take over your brain. Girl, what's wrong with you? Stop acting like a stalker! Plus, what would you say if he did speak to you? You see, he's with someone. Calm down, STOP overreacting, and STOP acting like an idiot because that man hasn't said a word to you. You're acting like a teenager when you only had one brief conversation with him. I sighed and shook my head. Was I having a conversation with myself again? I gathered myself and walked into the building.

Every day at work, my thoughts constantly dwelled on Everett. I couldn't understand why I was so obsessed with him and why I allowed him to run wild in my mind. Yes, he was attractive, but I knew I had to control the loneliness that lingered in my soul. I had to let it go! In my current state of hopelessness, it would be reckless of me to pursue a virtual stranger I barely knew. For all I knew, Everett was just like all the other men I'd met. I had to stop wasting time thinking about him. He'd make the first move if he were interested.

It was now Friday, and I hadn't seen Everett all week. A familiar despondency crept into my heart. My work week had been long and exhausting. I was tired and looked forward to going home. Although I knew I needed to stop thinking about Everett, seeing him in the building would have been nice. Resignedly, I gathered my belongings, locked my office door, and headed out. Each day, I deliberately walked toward the guard station, hoping he was there talking with Mr. Shelton.

As I approached the exit doors, I spotted Everett leaving

with the young woman I'd seen him with on Monday. I knew it was stupid, but I felt disappointed that I wasn't the woman with him. I quickly turned and walked in a different direction. Suddenly, I heard someone calling my name. I turned to see Everett approaching.

"Michelle! Michelle! What's the rush? How are you? I haven't seen you around in a while."

I did my best to appear calm and collected. Of course, you haven't. It's not like you've been looking for me.

"No rush," I replied. "I'm good. Just trying to beat the gridlock in the garage."

"Yeah, I was doing the same, but I left my cellphone in the office. By the way, are you going to the event?"

"Honestly, I haven't given it a second thought. What about you? Are you going?"

"Not this year. I have plans."

Then why did you ask? I wondered. You couldn't come up with a better conversation?

"Yes, I'm pretty certain I'm not going either."

"I understand," Everett said. "By the way, I'm having some people over for dinner this Saturday. If you're not too busy, you're more than welcome to come. Here's my business card. Call me if you decide to come, and I'll give you directions."

"Okay, I'll let you know. Have a good evening."

Gripping the card like it was the Holy Grail, I could have moonwalked to my car. I couldn't believe what had just happened. Feeling uplifted, I began to softly chant, "I got Everett's number! I got his number!" Then, the voice of reason slipped into my mind. Here you go again, getting all in your head. Slow down. It's just dinner, not a date. I got in my car, turned on the radio, and grooved to the music all the way home.

~

When I arrived home, the excitement in my heart immediately dissipated, and memories of failed relationships flooded my mind. Although I had a beautiful home, the lack of love and laughter blared like a fire alarm. I dropped my things on the floor and went to the kitchen to retrieve a bottle of Belvedere vodka from the freezer. After I poured a drink, I took it and the bottle to my bedroom. I didn't bother undressing. I turned on the TV, reached for the joint I smoked the night before, and lit it. After I took a few deep puffs, my phone buzzed. I saw that it was my mom. I knew if I didn't answer, she'd keep calling.

"Hi, Mom, what's going on?"

"Not much, sweetie. I was just calling to see how you're doing."

"I'm good. Had a long day at work. I'm tired and was thinking of taking a nap."

"Okay, when you get up, give me a call. Maybe we can grab a bite to eat later."

"Sure, Mom. I'll call you later."

I knew I wasn't going to return her call. I just wasn't in the mood for dinner or conversation. All I wanted was to drift off to sleep with my drink and joint and not think about anyone. One last hit, one last sip. Sleep, be my friend. Please take me to a place of no memories and silence, and let this night end.

As brilliant sunshine streamed through my bedroom window the next day, I felt the weight of a mild hangover from the weed and vodka. I reached for my cellphone, on the nightstand. I squinted at the clock and noticed it was after 10 a.m. No way was I ready to get up, so I slid my phone back onto the nightstand. Noticing Everett's business card, I picked it up and stared at it. I wanted to accept the dinner invitation, but I had a checklist of tasks I needed to do. Was it too early to call Everett, or should I wait? It would be magical to hear his voice this morning.

I decided to call Everett and let him know I couldn't attend. I knew it was silly, but I wondered what I'd say when he answered the phone. Girl, relax, and call the man! Can't you get out of your head for even a minute? I sat up against the pillows and tapped out Everett's number. It rang several times. Damn! He wasn't picking up. Shit, voicemail! I cleared my throat, took a deep breath, and waited for the beep.

"Hi, Everett. This is Michelle. Thanks for the invite, but I'm going to pass on dinner. Have a nice weekend."

Since I had no desire to get out of bed, I pulled the covers over my head and went back to sleep.

It seemed like I'd barely closed my eyes when the phone rang. Damnit, why didn't I turn off the ringer? As I fumbled for my phone, I knocked the damn thing on the floor. Shit, just let the call go to voicemail! Oh no, I can't do that! It might be Everett.

"Hello, hello?" I mumbled groggily.

"Hi, Michelle, this is Everett. I got your message. Sorry to hear you're not coming."

What, huh? Girl, get yourself together! It's Everett! You know how to speak English, remember?

I didn't want him to hear me moving around in bed, so I quickly sat up.

"Oh, hi, Everett. Yeah, I can't come. I had a super busy week, and honestly, I just want to relax this weekend and binge-watch something on Netflix."

"I understand. Well, if you're not busy next weekend, why don't you come over for a home-cooked meal?"

"That sounds wonderful. Let's see how the work week unfolds."

"Fair enough. Have a great relaxing Saturday, and I

hope you find something entertaining to watch. But, if you don't find something good, you're more than welcome to come."

"Thanks, but I need some chill time."

"Okay. Talk soon, Michelle."

I hung up and fell back on the bed with an enormous smile on my face. Immediately, I called my girlfriend, Jennifer.

"Girl, you're not going to believe this! I met a guy at work. His name is Everett, and he just invited me to his house next weekend for dinner."

"What are you going to do?"

"Girl, you know I'm going!"

"Okay, just be careful, Michelle," Jennifer warned. "You don't know him that well, and you recently ended a relationship. Please take it slow."

"Hold on," I said as I checked a text that popped up on my phone. "He just messaged me. Dinner at four next Saturday. OMG! He just assumed I was going to accept his invitation. What do I do? Do I respond now or wait a few hours?"

"Don't respond! What makes him think you're going to accept his invitation? Girl, there's more to this man. Just be wise and not foolish."

"I told you, Jennifer, he's very confident. We both know I'm going to his house for dinner. I may not go now, but I'm going."

"Okay, Michelle, if that's what you want."

"This is what I need. I got this, don't worry. Love you. Chat later."

It was interesting how I could talk to Jennifer far more openly than my family. My bestie and I grew up on the same block and had been friends since we were four. While I was four months older, Jennifer was definitely wiser. She was more of a sister than a friend, and we'd always been there for each other. We respected each other's space, and judging each other's actions didn't exist in our relationship. We respectfully expressed our opinions, and it was up to either of us to listen or not. This was one of the many reasons why I truly loved her.

Still feeling somewhat drunk, I turned off the ringer, pulled the covers over my head, and went back to sleep.

When I woke up a few hours later, I felt like someone had used my head as a punching bag. I slowly got out of bed and shuffled downstairs to make some coffee.

The coffee revived me, so I texted Everett. Hi, Everett. I'm not going to commit to dinner. Next week, I'm conducting training for the region. Let's see how it goes. When he didn't reply, I immediately got all in my head. Did I just blow my chance to be with him? Stop it, girl! You think way too much. Just let it go!

Chapter Five

Just as I expected, with regional training, the work week was hectic and mentally draining. It was the usual routine of going to work, going home, and starting over the next day. Yes, I thoroughly enjoyed my job, but there was nothing but a void outside of work. While I had a successful career, I lived an isolated, insular existence with little excitement. Another Friday, and nothing to do. Oh well, I decided I might as well head home and do what I've done since my breakup with Chase: pick up dinner, watch a movie, and sip some wine.

I gathered my belongings and left my office. As I approached the parking garage, as fate would have it, I noticed Everett's in his car waiting in line to exit. My first instinct was to wave, but then I thought there was no way he'd see me. I certainly didn't want to make a fool of myself again, so I continued to my car.

While I debated where to pick up a meal, my mind drifted to Everett. I glanced into the rearview mirror to see if his car was still in line. It would have made my day if he'd seen me and waved, considering he never responded to my text message. Had I read too much into everything?

Maybe he wasn't that interested in getting to know me. Of course, the more I brooded over it, the more upset I got. Thinking of my lonely life, I began to cry.

A few minutes later, I composed myself and drove to my favorite vegan restaurant to pick up my traditional Friday evening meal—an impossible burger with baked sweet potato fries, salad, and unsweetened iced tea. When I arrived home, I placed my meal on the kitchen counter and went to my room to change into a pair of sweats and a T-shirt. As I hung up my clothes, I noticed a black bag in the rear of the closet. Hesitating momentarily, I reached for the bag and opened it. Inside was Chase's jacket and ball cap. As tears welled in my eyes, I wondered why I hadn't noticed the bag before. I stared at the items and pondered if he'd left the bag on purpose. Was it a ploy to make me call him and beg for his forgiveness for not agreeing to wait?

Now I felt angry. No more tears! If that asshole thought his dirty trick would work, I had news for him—it wouldn't! I angrily snatched the bag out of the closet and stormed down to the garage. With almost sadistic glee, I crammed it into the trash bin. For damn sure, I didn't need those memories tormenting me this evening. I was feeling miserable enough. I retrieved my meal from the kitchen and sat down on the loveseat in the den to eat.

As I watched a comedy, my phone buzzed. It was a text from Everett.

Hey, Michelle, what are you doing?

I'm just relaxing and watching a movie.

How was your week?

Hectic.

I was thinking, if you're not busy tomorrow, why don't

you come over for that home-cooked meal I suggested? I've had a busy week and would love to have some company and enjoy a movie together.

That sounds great! What time?

How about 5ish?

Okay, I'll see you tomorrow. Text me your address.

~

I smiled. Damn, girl, you caved. I had to call Jennifer and tell her what had happened. My hands shook as I tapped out her number.

"Hi, Jennifer. Girl, I caved."

"What do you mean you caved?"

"Remember I told you Everett invited me over for dinner? Initially, I didn't accept. I told him we should wait and see how the work week unfolded. Well, I was just watching a movie, and he texted me. He invited me, and I accepted."

"Yep, you caved, all right," Jennifer said.

"I know I should have declined," I said, "considering that he didn't respond to my text. But right now, I need to enjoy the company of a man."

"I understand, Michelle, but is this what you want at this stage in your life? Your career is on track, and you're finally getting your life back together."

"I've had time to get over Chase, and I'm ready."

"Well, he's certainly persistent," Jennifer said.

"Yes, he is. He exudes confidence, and I find that quite charming. He knows what he wants, and he obviously wants me," I said with a giggle.

Jennifer chuckled, "Girl, you're too much."

"Jennifer, I know you're concerned and think I'm moving too fast. I'm not. You don't have to worry. As I said, I'm over Chase, and it's time for me to move forward."

"Okay, okay, you know the drill. Text me his full name and address. You don't know him that well, and I need to know your location, so make sure you turn on your phone's GPS tracker. This way, I'll know where you are and when you get home."

"Okay. Love you, girl. Chat later."

When the day came to go to Everett's house, I was excited and a little nervous. I paused, looked in the mirror, and wondered if I was wasting my time. In my heart, I longed for a husband because I was wary and tired of dating men. Being physically fit, I debated what to wear for hours. I wanted a sexy look but wanted to leave something to his imagination. Since it was just dinner at his house, there was no need to over-dress. I settled on a lavender and white cropped sweatshirt with jogging pants. After I finished preparing, I let my natural curls flow down my back. Before I left, I texted Jennifer Everett's contact details and turned on my phone's GPS tracker.

Driving through Everett's neighborhood, I was surprised and more than a little impressed at how upscale it was. His house was even more of a shock and certainly earned a "wow" reaction. His lovely two-story home had a double garage and was tastefully painted in subtle shades of gray, white, and rustic brown and trimmed with multi-colored bricks. The yard was immaculate, with perfectly trimmed grass and an array of beautiful flowers and shrubs. A pair of attic windows that conjured the image of a house from a famous horror movie captured my gaze. I laughed and hoped the house wouldn't be equally as haunted.

I parked in the driveway and walked up the stairs to the entrance. Seeing the front door slightly ajar, I rang the doorbell and stepped back to admire the neighborhood. This was not your typical cookie-cutter neighborhood. Each home was unique in size and style. From the pristine look of a few front yards, it seemed like the residents were competing for the Best Garden award. There was also no shortage of expensive cars parked in the driveways. As I turned, I noticed Everett approaching with a glass of wine. I couldn't help but smile. He was certainly prepared.

"Hi, Michelle! Please come in. I know you like wine, so I took the liberty and poured you a glass of Riesling."

"Thank you, Everett," I said, taking a sip of the slightly sweet wine. "It's lovely."

"I thought you'd like it."

"Oh, you did?" I smiled. "You thought I'd like it, or did you just play it safe?"

Everett laughed and escorted me inside. As I entered his home, the smell of pumpkin spice lingered in the air, and I was more than a little blown away by the tasteful furnishings and decorations. I immediately noticed an eclectic collection of mirrors almost everywhere I looked. I wondered why he had so many. Were the mirrors placed so that he could see virtually every angle of the house? Was he so vain that he looked at himself all the time, or were they placed so that he could watch others without them realizing it?

"Everett, your home is stunning! I love that blue, yellow, and gray oversized sectional. The colors accentuate the rustic flooring and set the tone for comfort."

"Thanks. I put a lot of love and money into this place."

"Did you hire a decorator, or did you do it?"

"I needed to bounce my ideas off a professional, so I did both."

"The ambiance is divine. So warm and relaxing."

"Comfort was the plan," he said. "On that note, it's beautiful outside. Why don't we go out to the deck?"

"That sounds wonderful."

Drink in hand, I followed Everett through the dining room and out a pair of French doors onto a wooden multi-level privacy deck that stepped from the pages of an architectural magazine. The deck had a retractable awning, a built-in kitchen, a jacuzzi, a fireplace, and seating for eight. Everett led me toward a light blue cushioned loveseat and sat beside me.

"Looks like you need a refill," he offered.

"I'm good for now. Maybe later."

"I know I promised you a home-cooked meal, but a friend told me about this quaint family-style Mediterranean restaurant in The District and said the food is amazing. I thought we could order and pick it up," he suggested. "What do you think?"

"Well, I was actually looking forward to a home-cooked meal."

"Oh, no problem. I can cook."

"I'm just kidding. I love Mediterranean food. And if it's fine with you, I'd rather go out to eat."

"Okay, then we'll go out."

As I sat overlooking Everett's backyard, I admired the beautiful landscaping. Comfortable seating added an elegant touch to a fire pit in the left corner of the yard. I imagined sipping freshly brewed coffee on the deck in the morning, listening to the serenade of birds, and hearing the cool breeze rustling through the trees. I watched the birds flutter into the sky and wondered if Everett and I would soar toward love and a shared future.

"Michelle?"

Lost in thought, I never realized Everett was talking to me. I felt like a foolish teenager sitting next to my high school crush.

"Are you okay? You seemed a million miles away."

"Sorry," I said. "Your yard is so serene. I just got lost in the peacefulness. But it must be quite a task to maintain."

"Yes, it's a lot of work, so I have a landscaping company take care of it," Everett said proudly. "I love sitting outside after a long day at work. It's so relaxing."

"I know what you mean," I said. "I love sitting on my patio with a glass of wine. That's how I decompress after a long day at work."

Everett nodded. "Well, we have that in common."

"Yes, we do," I said with a smile.

Everett glanced at my empty glass. "I see you finished your drink. Ready to leave?"

"Sure, I just need to freshen up."

Everett gathered the glasses. I followed him indoors, and he directed me toward the guest bathroom. I couldn't help imagining what it would be like to wake up every morning with Everett by my side. I envisioned cooking together and enjoying our meals on the deck or just spending time stargazing with a glass of wine.

Was I foolish to be thinking this way so soon? Was I about to ignore every bitter relationship lesson I learned? I left the bathroom and noticed Everett standing near the stairs with car keys in hand.

"Ready to go?" he asked.

"Yes, I am."

∾

Everett led me to the garage, where a late model gray metallic BMW sedan was parked. Unlike most garages that acted mostly as junk storage, it was immaculately organized. Always the gentleman, Everett opened the door for me. While the garage door rolled open, he started the car. I almost jumped out of my seat from the shock of blaring rock music.

"I'm so sorry!" he said, quickly lowering the volume. "Sometimes I like to play my music loud. When I hear the right song, it just takes me to another place."

"No problem!" I laughed lightly. "I remember those days in college."

As we drove through the neighborhood, Everett opened the sunroof. I listened to the music and stared out the window taking in the cool breeze.

"You, okay?" Everett asked.

"Great. Just enjoying the ride," I smiled. "It's nice having someone drive me around."

Everett glanced at me. "Oh, so I'm your private driver?"

"For this evening, at least."

"I don't mind driving around a beautiful woman."

About fifteen minutes later, we arrived at the restaurant. Everett got out and came to open the door. As he helped me out, I had to admit I enjoyed the attention as no one had treated me like this in quite a while.

Chapter Six

The storefront Mediterranean restaurant had a genuine traditional Middle Eastern vibe. As we walked inside, the music and the wonderful cooking aromas ushered in fond memories of the year I spent in Turkey. As we stood in the reception area, a swarthy young man with rumpled ebony hair wearing a black pullover, jeans, and a rumpled apron, greeted us with a friendly smile. He took two menus and directed us to a table.

Although the wall decor was authentic, the restaurant itself was painted an institutional gray with furniture better suited for a cafeteria. A battered drinks cooler rattled near the entrance. While the interior was far from appealing, I prayed the food would be amazing.

As Everett perused the menu, I noticed the clientele was almost entirely Middle Eastern men. The only other women besides me were the cashier and an older woman with her son at a table near the door. I knew it was wrong but became uncomfortable and avoided eye contact.

"Everett, did you notice that there are almost no women here?"

"What are you talking about?" Everett said still perusing the menu.

"Do you think it's safe here?" I whispered. "It doesn't look like a place I'd like to come to at night."

"Babe, can you stop? I don't like it when you talk like this."

"Did your friends eat here or order to go?"

"I don't know. They just said the food was good. Just relax and look at the menu."

While I tried to focus on the menu, I couldn't help but notice the men from the corner of my eye. I should have known better than to stereotype, but I didn't feel comfortable. None spoke English, and I began to feel uncomfortable. I put my menu down.

"Everett, are you sure you want to stay here? Maybe we should go somewhere else?"

Everett shook his head. "Honestly, Michelle, you need to get out of your head. No more political thrillers for you. Let's order."

The calmness in his eyes soothed me. I began to feel a little foolish and thought about how I felt when others stereotyped me.

Everett signaled the young man. I ordered hummus with garlic and tandoori naan, lamb chops with vegetable biryani, and a side salad. Everett ordered the shrimp curry, goat karahi, a salad, and two Mythos beers.

When the young man returned with our beers, I took a few sips and started to calm down.

"Feeling better now?" Everett asked. "Do you still feel like you need to run for your life?"

I sheepishly shook my head. "I'm okay."

"Glad to hear it. So how was your work week?"

"As the senior specialist, I'm always busy. That's why I look forward to the weekends so I can relax."

"I can relate. My job is non-stop. I enjoy the work, but

there are days when I feel like throwing the computer out of the window," he said with a laugh.

I laughed, too, and felt my tension drain away. "Yeah, I've had a few of those days. Other than work, what are your hobbies?"

"I enjoy cooking and reading," Everett stated. "On rainy days, I light the fireplace, cook a meal, sit back with a book, and enjoy the evening. Not to brag, but I'm a damn good cook, and before you say it," he laughed and leaned forward in his chair, "I'll definitely cook you a meal."

"Hopefully, I'll have the pleasure of watching Chef Everett work his magic."

Everett tapped his beer bottle against mine. "You most definitely will."

As we talked, the young man returned with our food. I almost swooned from the intoxicating aroma. The lamb was fabulous and melted in my mouth. Appreciating the succulent flavor and savory seasoning, I regretted my earlier behavior and realized how simple it was to jump to conclusions. Noticing my blissful expression, Everett smiled.

"Enjoying the food?" Everett put a forkful of shrimp curry in his mouth.

"It's delicious!"

"Oh, it's delicious?" he echoed sarcastically. "You know some of the best food is found in places like this."

I rolled my eyes. "Okay, but something still could have happened. I'm just glad it didn't."

We finished our meal. While I ate everything ordered, Everett took the rest of his food home in a box.

Afterward, we decided to take a walk around the area. There wasn't much to see as the restaurant was located in a business district. I didn't mind because I was engrossed in my conversation with Everett. We walked around for about thirty minutes before we returned to the car. When we returned to his place, I looked at my watch and noticed it was after nine-thirty.

"Everett, today was wonderful!" I declared. "Thanks so much for dinner. I guess I should head home."

"What's the rush?" he asked, pulling into the garage.

"No rush."

"Cool! Then let's have and drink and let me introduce you to Spice."

Puzzled, I asked. "Spice?"

Everett chuckled. "You'll see soon enough."

I was bouncing with curiosity. I followed Everett into the house. He led me to the basement to a room displaying a sign above the door that read, "Everett's Play Room."

"Is this your man cave, or is it Spice?" I asked as he opened the door and motioned me inside.

"It's a very special man cave. If you're not afraid to enter, please come in."

As I brushed past Everett, the scent of his cologne beckoned me closer. With all the strength and self-control I could muster, I kept moving. It was certainly going to be an interesting night.

As I entered the man cave, I felt like I'd walked into an upscale pool hall. The neon sign above the bar, which read Everett's Sport's Bar - Relax - Drinks on the House, set the cool vibe for the room. I was certain Everett noticed the surprise on my face when I looked around.

I paused. "Okay, Everett, what's going on?"

Pointing at the pool table, Everett said, "Michelle, I'd like to introduce you to Spice."

"Are you kidding? Really, you named your pool table Spice?"

"Yes, because once I whoop that ass, you're not going to be happy with Spice. So go ahead and touch her, talk to her, and maybe you and she will turn out to be good friends. But I have to warn you, she can get jealous."

By now, I was laughing hysterically. So, I played his little game and said, "Sounds good to me. But I must warn you and Spice, I'm a damn good pool player, so you better bring you're A-game!"

"Oh, it's like that, is it?" he remarked.

I laughed. "Always."

Spice sat in the center of the room, illuminated by a light fixture designed with cue balls and three cone-shaped pendants with matching chains. A display of six multicolored pool sticks graced the wall.

Toward the rear of the room, a wraparound orange, blue, and gray retro-style bar with six orange swivel Longneck barstools added sparkle to the décor. A wall-mounted 50-inch television behind the bar was angled to be viewed from anywhere in the room. But the crown jewels were the authentic popcorn machine and jukebox.

"This is fantastic, Everett! I love the jukebox!"

"It gets even better," he boasted. "I can operate it using my phone."

He retrieved his phone from his pocket. With a swipe, old-school hip-hop bounced off of the walls. With the music reverberating in my soul, I snapped my fingers and swayed to the beat.

Everett pointed to a rack of pool cues and said, "Choose your stick."

While I made my selection, he went to the bar and

poured two shots of Patrón. He's trying to get me drunk, I thought. What he doesn't know is that I can handle my liquor. He handed me the glass with a slice of lime. We downed the shots together, and it went straight to my head.

I gave him a challenging look. "Let's play."

I was having so much fun, and after a couple more shots of Patrón, I forgot about the time. We played one game, and while we played, Everett started flirting with me. So, this is your modus operandi? Well, I had to at least credit him with some ingenuity, so, I let him play his little game. He purposely bumped against me and grabbed me to distract me. His body pressing against me felt good. Too good. My mind warned me to leave, but my body shouted at me to stay.

Everett watched me with admiration. "Damn, Michelle, you weren't kidding. You're a great player!"

I simply smiled and took my next shot, which ended the game.

Everett grinned. "Well, now we have a problem. No way can I let you beat me in a game of pool in my house. Rack them up!"

I laughed. "I won, so loser racks."

"No problem."

Everett racked the balls, and I took the first shot. Not to brag, but I made an exceptional break, and the first ball in the hole was solid. This time, Everett stepped up his game and still lost!

Laughing, I said, "So, I guess Spice is tired of the same old games."

"Oh, oh, okay. That's all right, sweet lady. You were a distraction. But just know, I'm coming for you."

"Well, I have to give you credit. Your game did improve, just not enough to beat me."

"That's fine. Go ahead and brag, but don't let your guard down because the games have just begun, and I'm a man with many talents."

"Well, Mr. Many Talents, bring it on! Oh, and by the way, you might want to wipe Spice's tears."

We laughed as we placed our cue sticks back on the wall rack.

~

"Michelle, it's getting late, and we've had a few drinks," Everett said. "If you like, you're more than welcome to spend the night in the guest room, or if you're not afraid, we can play another game."

In the guest room? Really? Girl, you barely know this man. Don't be reckless. Take your ass home! Why was I talking to myself again? But I couldn't silence that nagging voice. You know you just got out of a relationship. You're vulnerable. Think about what you're doing!

"What's on your mind?" he asked, noticing my distraction.

"Ah, nothing."

"You don't have to worry," he said. "I promise I won't do anything you don't want me to."

My resistance fading, I smiled. "Sure, I'll stay."

"Another game or sleep?"

"I'm somewhat tired, and the Patrón got my head spinning."

"Okay. Let me get you something to sleep in." Everett left the room.

Okay, don't judge. He got me to stay the night, but there was no way in HELL I was ending up in his bed. At least, that's what I kept telling myself while my body screamed at him to touch me. Girl, pull yourself together. Stop acting like a silly child. Step back and look at what you're doing! If you sleep with him on the first date, what will he think of you? You don't know him that well. For damn sure, it's not going to end in your favor. Leave! Leave now, and stop playing this game of cat and mouse!

Everett returned with one of his T-shirts and a plush robe and showed me to the guest room.

"You should be comfortable in this."

The fabric of both felt sensual in my hand. My resolve was about to slide straight down the Grand Canyon.

"Thank you, Everett."

He led me to his guest room. Girl, what's wrong with you? Don't go any further! You don't see that he's planning on sleeping with you tonight? For once, have some self-respect!

"Goodnight," I murmured.

"Goodnight, Michelle," he said and turned to walk down the hall.

I was aching to cuddle up to Everett but didn't want my eagerness to show. Reluctantly, I opened the door and stepped into an exquisitely decorated guest room. The teal-painted walls were offset by a white ceiling and accented by a large painting of purple orchid flowers that hung on the wall above the bed. I kicked off my shoes and sank onto a queen-size bed covered with a white duvet and topped with four white pillows. The comforter was decadent, and I felt like I was at a luxurious resort.

I thought about Everett with a mix of hunger and admiration. Not only could he decorate, but his hospitality was impeccable. I plugged my phone into a Bluetooth speaker on the nightstand and selected some soothing zen music.

As I relaxed on the bed, I imagined Everett standing outside my door, longing to knock.

I turned down the music and listened hopefully, but I heard nothing. I rose and undressed, slipped on Everett's T-shirt, and draped my clothes over a vintage chrome clothes rack in the corner of the room. I noticed that Everett had left a shirt on it. I picked up the shirt, and when I held it close, it smelled of his cologne. Had he left it there on purpose? Heart racing, sweet spot throbbing, I grabbed one of the pillows, placed it between my legs, and drifted off to sleep.

The next morning, I woke up to the delicious aroma of cooking. I got up, dressed, and walked into the bathroom. Everett left toiletries and towels on the counter. Damn, he's good! I quickly washed up and made my way to the kitchen. Everett was at the stove cooking bacon, eggs, and hash browns. A plate of buttery, hot-from-the-oven biscuits waited on the counter. My mouth started watering.

"The biscuits smell wonderful!"

Everett grinned. "Thanks. I told you I was a good cook. How did you sleep?"

"Like a baby."

He approached and guided me to a contemporary faux marble dining table and pulled out a chair.

"Here's that home-cooked meal I promised you," he said, kissing me on the forehead.

I tried not to react to the kiss and struggled to regain my composure.

"Everett, I had a wonderful time yesterday."

"I'm glad to hear that. I wanted you to feel comfortable. I know you were concerned that I'd come to your room."

I burst out with a laugh. "No, I wasn't worried."

Everett lifted an eyebrow. "Really?"

"Yes, really."

As I waited for Everett to prepare my plate, I gazed at his toned, muscular body and imagined how it would feel to lay beside him. Damn, I needed to be held! Once again, I tried to reign in my emotions as he brought two plates to the table.

"Enjoy," he said, pouring coffee for us.

After breakfast, Everett suggested we sit on the deck. We spent the morning talking and laughing.

"Would you like a mimosa, Michelle?"

"Yes, please."

Everett went into the house and returned shortly with the mimosas and two shots of Patrón and lime.

I leaned back and looked at him. "Patrón?"

"Can you handle a shot, or is it too early for you?" He shrugged his shoulders. "If it is, I'll understand."

"Oh, okay, you challenging me to a drink off? Just like I taught you and Spice a lesson last night, I'm going to do it again, but afterward, I really can't stay too long. I have things to do today."

"Are you sure?" He smirked at me.

"I'm sure."

We clinked our glasses, took the shots, and chased with the lime. So, he thought last night was the prelude to sex, and this morning he was going to unlock the door. Well, it wasn't going to happen.

We sat back, sipped our mimosas, and talked for a couple of hours, then I left. As I drove home, my phone rang.

"Hi, Everett."

"Hey, I just wanted to say how much I enjoyed spending

time with you," he said. "If you're not busy next weekend, why don't we get together?"

"Unfortunately, next weekend won't work," I replied. "I'll be on a business trip for a couple of weeks."

"Okay, maybe when you get back."

"That sounds like a plan," I said with a smile. "Let's chat later."

"Look forward to it," Everett said.

Chapter Seven

During my two-week business trip, speaking to Everett became the highlight of my day. We talked about our families, jobs, our interests outside of work, and how much we missed each other. I discovered we both enjoyed a stimulating conversation. Everett loved to read and often prompted a discussion. He was always surprised by my ability to engage and understand most topics. Sometimes, he thought he was slick and tried to catch me off guard, but it rarely worked. I always had something to contribute when presented with a challenge.

Being away from Everett felt like an eternity, and the thought of seeing him fueled my desire to be loved. I looked forward to the end of the second week and my Friday flight home. Although I enjoyed my time with him, I promised myself I wouldn't focus on marriage as I did in the past. My breakup with Chase was emotionally shattering, and I didn't want to carry the scars into my relationship with Everett. I felt it was best to allow the relationship to organically unfold.

When I returned, Everett called and suggested we

attend the summer jazz festival at Washington Square Park on Saturday.

"Everett, I'd love to attend, but honestly, the thought of using those nasty portable toilets has always put me off attending these events."

"I can't say I blame you," he agreed. "But why don't we at least check it out? We can leave when you want to go."

"Okay, that works," I said. "By the way, I missed you."

"Same here. Why don't you get some rest? I don't want you to be tired. I'll pick you up around five."

I gathered my bags and hauled them to the bedroom to unpack. I felt fatigued from the flight, so I left the unpacking for when I felt up to it. Instead, I treated myself to a long hot shower and washed my hair. I knew I shouldn't go to bed with wet hair, but honestly, I didn't have the energy to deal with drying and styling it, so I pulled my hair into a ponytail and put on a satin bonnet.

As I dried off, I looked at my naked body and imagined Everett's hands moving all over me. The fantasy fueled a deep desire to pleasure myself. I went to the bedroom, turned on the music, and sat on the bed. I took a couple of long drags from the joint on my nightstand. Feeling buzzed, I turned off the lights and imagined my hands were Everett's. It didn't take long before I climaxed.

I was so excited to see Everett that I tossed and turned all night and woke up around seven. Out of habit, I reached for my phone to check text messages and emails. I had several text messages, including one from Everett.

His message read, Hey babe, hope you slept well. I missed you so much when you were away. I'm glad you're back. Can't wait to see you today.

I rolled over in bed, placed my hand on my heart, and

smiled. He knew I'd be asleep when he sent the message. He wanted to be the first person I thought of when I woke up, and he succeeded. Content to stay in bed, I reached for the remote and turned on the TV. I flipped through the channels and finally settled on the news. The forecast for today would be in the high 90s. It was going to be a scorcher, so I'd wear shorts. Since I had a few more hours to spare, I went back to sleep.

Four hours later, I woke up feeling well-rested. I went to the bathroom to get ready. Thinking of the pleasure I received last night; I giggled as I stood naked in the bathroom. I slipped on my robe, went to the kitchen to make some coffee, and checked my computer. Fortunately, there was no urgent task that required my attention, so I logged off.

Since Everett wouldn't pick me up for a few hours, I made a mango protein shake and enjoyed it and my coffee under the canopy on the patio. Basking in the warmth, I expressed my gratitude to the universe for providing me with everything I needed. After finishing my breakfast, I went inside to prepare for my evening with Everett.

After I laid out my two-piece floral crop top short set on the bed, I went to the bathroom to complete my routine. In such heat, I didn't want my hair on my neck or face, so I pulled it into an updo ponytail and adorned it with a white-beaded hair stick. I finished my look with silver hoop earrings, silver bangles, a silver-beaded ankle bracelet, and silver sequin slip-on Muffin sneakers for comfort.

I was more than pleased when I inspected myself in the full-length mirror. I smiled. It was the perfect outfit to give Everett a peek at my toned stomach but still leave something to his imagination. To help me relax, I lit my joint and took a couple of drags before heading downstairs to wait for Everett. As I sat on my bed, my phone vibrated.

"Hi, Everett!"

"Hi, babe, I'm right around the corner. You ready?"

"Yes, I'll wait outside."

As soon as I stepped onto the porch, Everett pulled into the driveway. He slowly got out of the car. As usual, he was smartly dressed in a green two-piece sports short set with white sneakers. While he looked good, something about his energy was off.

I opened my front door. "Come on in," I said. It was only when he reached to kiss me that I noticed he was wearing braces.

"Everett, when did you get braces?"

He hugged me and smiled. "I got them last week. I'm getting used to them, but do my teeth ache!"

I noticed the slight fatigue on his face. While I never had braces, I had friends who did, and it was never a pleasant experience.

"Are you sure you're up to going?" I asked. "We can always reschedule our date."

"No, I'm good. A little wine and smoke before we leave will dull the pain."

"Okay. Let me hook you up."

Walking to the kitchen, I felt a thrill of excitement. Everett was handsome, but fixing his teeth would take him to a new level.

"Have a seat," I offered before going upstairs.

I grabbed a freshly rolled joint from the nightstand and realized I hadn't applied any perfume, so I quickly spritzed myself. The moment I returned to the kitchen, Everett sniffed appreciatively.

"You smell divine."

"Thanks," I said, lighting the joint. "It's an old favorite."

Everett took a couple of hits. I poured glasses of wine and sat beside him.

"How long do you have to wear them?" I asked.

"For about eighteen months, but it will be worth the aggravation. I've wanted to fix my teeth for a while now. I've just been putting it off."

At that moment, I knew I needed to conceal the burning desire to fall into his embrace and kiss the pain away.

"Well, if there's anything I can do to ease the pain, let me know."

The moment I saw the grin on Everett's face, I realized he knew exactly what I was offering. I watched his expression transform from the hits.

"Come here and open your mouth," he said.

I looked at him in puzzlement. "Why?"

"Trust me. Open your mouth."

I leaned over and opened my mouth. Everett took a drag of the joint and blew the smoke into it. Let's just say I damn near had an orgasm feeling his warm breath flowing from his mouth. I inhaled the smoke.

"Let me have another shot," I said, feeling a mild buzz. I inhaled again. "If we keep this up, we're not going to the event."

Everett grinned. "You're right. We better get going before something else happens."

"Good idea. You up to driving?"

"I'm fine. Since it's going to be so hot today, I brought folding chairs with attached umbrellas and a cooler filled with drinks and snacks."

"That's so thoughtful of you, Everett! Now I don't have to bring my umbrella."

"I just wanted to do something special as a welcome home gift."

Fighting the urge to blurt out how I felt about him, I responded with a simple, "Thanks, you're always so considerate."

He motioned to the front door. "Shall we go?"

The drive to the festival took about thirty minutes through town. Everett turned up the music to set the mood, and we both sang along to his mix of blues songs. We took the freeway, hoping to avoid traffic, but we got stuck as soon as we took the exit to the festival. The scene was chaotic, with people jaywalking everywhere while others respectfully waited at the crosswalk for the lights to change.

As we inched through the traffic, I rolled down the window to fully absorb the music blaring from the sound system. It reverberated in my soul, and the energy was contagious. Just like the crowd enthusiastically walking to the venue, I was overwhelmed by excitement and began to sway to the music while Everett tapped his hands on the steering wheel.

"Everett, I hope we find a place to park," I said, glancing at the jammed streets. "It's so crowded."

"No worries, my sweet, we will. I just hope it's not far from the venue."

It took about ten minutes to find a parking spot. We were fortunate. The lot charge was only twenty-five dollars and less than three blocks from the venue. I was glad I wore comfortable shoes because the last thing I wanted to deal with was aching feet.

As expected, the venue was packed. One area was sectioned off and lined with blue portable toilets. The reek from the chemicals was nauseating. I didn't want to appear difficult, so I marched on holding Everett's hand. As we searched for a place to set up, the smell of marijuana drifted in the air. Although I enjoyed the taste and smell of marijuana in a more intimate setting, I had no desire to sit next to people smoking it.

We scouted the perfect location toward the rear of the park surrounded by tall trees. We set up our chairs and enjoyed various jazz bands while having brief conversations, snacking, and sipping wine. As we watched the musicians, I noticed from the corner of my eye that Everett was smiling at me.

I looked at him. "I'm having a great time, Everett," I said.

"Same here. I'm glad you're enjoying yourself."

"This is just what I needed. Some good company and music."

"The music is fantastic," Everett said, swaying to the rhythm.

"Just the music?" I asked.

He smiled. Even with the braces, I could already see what a dazzling smile he'd have.

"Just kidding. You're the cherry on a very delicious cake."

I tilted my head and coyly glanced at him. "Am I the cherry on your cake?"

"Every day of the week, my sweet lady." His words felt like a sensual caress.

"Now there's some music to my ears," I said.

~

As the evening wore on, I could no longer ignore my throbbing bladder. I silently cursed. Damn, not now! I tried to force the urge from my mind, but of course, it didn't work.

After five minutes, I whispered to Everett, "I really need to go to the bathroom, but I just can't bring myself to use those nasty porta-potties."

"No worries, Michelle. Let's leave."

We gathered our things, and as we left the venue, I spotted a vegan vendor selling funnel cakes.

"Everett, I have to get one!"

"Are you sure? The line is kind of long, and I thought ..."

"I do have to go, but the line's moving. Why don't you get the car? I'll meet you at the entrance."

"Are you sure?"

"Yes."

"Okay, I'll be as quick as I can," he said, walking away.

I stood in line, trying unsuccessfully to ignore my bursting bladder. Of course, the line moved like a glacier. I was about ready to walk away when I finally reached the counter. Practically sprinting to the parking lot entrance, I could have cried with relief to see Everett waiting.

"Drive!" I yelled as I jumped in the car.

Everett gassed it, and a moment later, he made a sharp left turn and pulled up to a hotel.

"Why are you stopping here?" I yelled.

"The bathroom here should be clean enough," he said.

I fidgeted uncomfortably as Everett parked close to the entrance.

"I've never used the bathrooms at a hotel I wasn't staying in," I said. "Do I just walk in like a guest?"

"I've done it before," Everett stated. "Honestly, the staff is so busy most of the time, they won't know if you're staying there or visiting someone."

By now, I was squirming, so I jumped out of the car and took off. As I ran, I tripped over a step and almost pissed my pants. As I got up, Everett was running toward me and grabbed my arm.

"Are you okay?"

"Yes," I said, trying to conceal my embarrassment.

Fortunately, I spotted a bathroom inside the lobby. The receptionist was busy with a guest and didn't even glance up. It was all I could do to keep from running, but I had to maintain some decorum. When I returned to the car, Everett burst into laughter.

"Don't get mad," he snickered. "But you took off like a bat out of hell! When you went down, it was like a scene from a comedy! You hit the ground and bounced straight up! I hope you didn't hurt yourself."

~

Now that my bladder wasn't on the verge of exploding, I saw the humor of the situation.

"I'm okay. It's always easier for men," I remarked, cocking an eyebrow at him. "But gravity doesn't quite work the same way for women."

Everett burst into laughter again. Replaying the scene in my mind, I also burst into laughter. We laughed until we were practically in tears.

"Everett, I can't remember the last time I laughed so hard! Thank you for bringing laughter back to my life again."

Still chuckling, Everett pulled out of the hotel parking lot. As he drove, I ate my funnel cake, and yes, after all that, it was delicious.

When we arrived at my place, Everett got out of the car and opened my door. He helped me out of the car and pulled me into a gentle kiss. His lips were silky, and his tongue was a bold explorer in my mouth. Damn, what was he doing to me? I know it's been a while, but DAMN!

"Michelle, today was magical."

"It certainly was," I whispered, struggling to compose myself.

Everett gazed longingly into my eyes. "Babe, if I don't leave now, I'm going to kiss you again. Have a good night, and let's talk tomorrow."

"I understand," I nodded and reluctantly walked to my door.

Though I desperately wanted to look back, I knew if I did, I would have invited him in. I slowly walked toward the house so Everett could have one last look at me before I shut the door.

Mirror, Mirror on the wall, I felt as though I'd lost faith in love. Authenticity in my past relationships was superficial, and I dealt with insincere men too weak to deal with difficult truths, leaving me with the jagged remnants of broken mirrors. Mirror, I saw the reflection of your eyes and wondered whose eyes I had been looking through. Was this love real or just another fantasy in my mind? Or was his love the reality of this place in time?

Mirror, I never expected to fall for a man I hardly knew, but he made me forget the reality I tried to ignore and reassured me that his heart was true. After I met him, my heart rejoiced. The warmth of his dark eyes welcomed me, and his gentle kiss banished my loneliness to the dying rays of a setting sun. I never would have imagined that we would evolve beyond friends, but he conquered the doubts in my heart.

He cared deeply for me and enjoyed the physical and emotional attention I gave. Emboldened, casting caution aside, I sailed deeper into his mesmerizing love. Our hearts beat in synchronicity, and his voice lived in the depths of my soul. After our first passionate kiss, he whispered that he loved everything about me. He filled the void in my heart that I had kept hidden for so long. I knew he'd take my hand and lead me to an enchanted land as beautiful as a living dream.

Over time, I witnessed the gentleness of a boy and the strength of a man. For once in my life, I allowed our love to organically unfold. Meeting him changed my life for the better, but I feared his rejection if I expressed how much he meant to me. So at this moment in time, I embraced patience and enjoyed the beautiful scenery of our love. Mirror, Mirror on the wall, I had finally found the love I'd always dreamed of.

Chapter Eight

Over the next few months, Everett and I were inseparable, like souls bonded from the beginning of time. We often sat on his deck for hours listening to music, drinking, smoking marijuana, and talking. Our space consisted of him and me draped by a dazzling vista of twinkling stars. We were in the friendship stage of our relationship but still without sex. I knew in my heart that Everett wondered if or when it would happen. However, I wasn't holding sex hostage. I simply needed more time to get to know him.

Everett considered my feelings and always opened my doors, held my hand, and walked next to the curb to protect me. If I'd slept with him on the first date, would he have taken the time to develop true feelings for me or just deleted me from his contacts? Statistics have proven that men were less likely to call a woman after sex on the first date, which was a risk I wasn't willing to take. I was fully aware of myself, totally in control of my mind and body, and knew I made the correct decision not to dive into bed with him. The love in my head and heart yearned for much more from him, but logic reminded me to be patient.

Time allowed me to discover that Everett was athletic, highly competitive, and enjoyed playing basketball, golf, and racquetball. He often went to the gym and played basketball with his friends and invited me to go with him. Sometimes, I sat and watched his body effortlessly run up and down the court for a while before I left to complete my workout. Everett felt it was important for us to be active and in good health. Unlike most men I dated, he was sincerely interested in getting to know what I liked and disliked. He often said that my happiness was important to him because if he knew what gave me pleasure, then it would be easy for him to satisfy me.

The tenderness of Everett's heart was always on display. It was as if he could see right through me. At the end of most workdays, I was mentally exhausted and needed to wind down, and all I dreamed about was going to Everett's house to relax. Now that Friday had arrived, it was a completely different routine from picking something up to eat and having a date night with wine and the TV. Tonight, I was going to Everett's place.

Since he knew I was coming over, he left the front door unlocked. When I arrived, I found him sitting outside on the deck. Fatigued, I poured a glass of wine and went to join him. When I opened the patio door, Everett looked surprised and quickly put down his phone. Immediately, I thought, Here we go. Does he have something to hide? I knew that shouldn't have been my first thought, but I'd seen this behavior in the past. I pretended I didn't notice his reaction.

I went to kiss him and sat down.

"How was your day, babe?" he asked.

"Exhausting. I'm glad this work week is over."

"What have you been up to?"

"Not much," Everett said. "When I got home, I turned on some music and relaxed with a drink and a joint. Want a hit?"

"Sure."

He took a hit and passed it to me. I leaned back in the chair, took a long hit, and slowly exhaled. Damn, just what I needed after a long day.

"Babe, I know what you need." Everett removed my shoes and massaged my feet.

"That feels wonderful!" I murmured.

I closed my eyes and tried to relax, but his behavior when I walked onto the deck replayed in my mind. I tried to rationalize what had happened. Maybe he was playing a game on his phone or just reading an e-mail and wanted to give me his undivided attention. Everett and I were in a good place and attempting to build a relationship. Since we were still in the friendship stage, there was no point in creating problems, so I just relegated what happened to the far recesses of my mind.

Everett was good to me and often did unexpected things like massaging my feet because he loved seeing me smile. And I did the same. It was the first time I felt so comfortable in a relationship. There was never a dull moment with him, and our relationship was filled with love, laughter, and pranks.

For example, I found Everett in the shower when I arrived for one of my evening sleepovers in the guest room. I decided to hide in the laundry room. I turned off the hallway lights and waited for him to walk by. When he did,

I jumped out, but things didn't go as planned. He yelled, and his towel fell to the floor. Immediately, my eyes riveted on his more than the generous package. Let's just say, damn!

"Girl, what's wrong with you?" he gasped. "I could have hurt you!"

As he retrieved the towel, I just stared at him with an intense desire to have him deep inside of me. And by the glorious rise of his sunshine, he felt the same. To break up the awkwardness, we both started laughing hysterically. I was practically in tears and only stopped when my stomach cramped.

"Now you know I'm going to get your ass," he smirked.

I threw up my hands defensively. "I was just playing with you!"

"I know, but you better sleep with one eye open. You know I'm competitive, and I'm going to get you."

Everett eventually got me back, but not how I expected. One night when I stayed at his place, I decided to wash my hair. With thick hair, I found it easier to wash my hair in the shower. I followed my routine of shampooing my hair and letting the conditioner soak in while I scrubbed myself. As I stood there enjoying the hot water splashing on my body, I opened the shower curtain and reached for a disposable plastic shower cap I used to allow deeper conditioning of my hair. When I finished my shower and dried off, I put on my bathrobe and went to talk to Everett for a few minutes while I waited for the conditioner to work on my hair.

I was a little tired, so I told Everett I was going to lie down before I rinsed out the conditioner. I went to the bedroom, turned out the lights, slipped beneath the covers, and snuggled against the pillow. Suddenly, I felt something slimy, wet, hard, and sharp. Paralyzed with fear, I was afraid to move. My heart felt as though it would burst out of my chest. I didn't know why I was whispering to myself, but I was. Get up, Michelle, get up! Finally, I screamed, jumped out of bed, and turned on the lights. With shaky hands, I pulled back the covers. I saw a lobster shell. What the fuck!

"Everett!" I yelled.

All I heard was laughter. When I opened the door, he was practically rolling on the floor.

"I warned you I was going to get you, and the leftover lobster shell was the perfect weapon!"

As I reached to shove him, he took off, so I chased him around the house. Suddenly, he grabbed me, pulled me to the floor, and began kissing me.

"Everett, stop!"

"Now you know you don't want me to do that," he whispered.

"Yes, I do! I need to rinse the conditioner out of my hair."

"It can wait, beautiful."

"Everett, if this is how our practical jokes are going to end, you can prank me anytime!"

Three months into our deepening friendship, Everett had yet to make any sexual advances toward me. He adored me, and I was beginning to fall in love with him. Although he hadn't asked me to be his girlfriend, I knew it would only be a matter of time. I felt as though I'd given the relationship time to develop into a friendship that stimulated the mind and body. If he initiated sex, I was ready.

When it finally happened, Everett and I were cuddling

in the dark on his oversized chaise lounge in the family room. We were watching a thriller on TV, but my mind was more focused on how making love to him the first time would feel. I inhaled deeply, snuggled closer to him, and slowly exhaled. Oh, his irresistible smell! I want him all over me! I struggled to retain my composure. Focus, Michelle, don't make the first move. I tried to stem my emotions by eating my popcorn.

Suddenly, I caught fleeting motion from the corner of my eye. I screamed and leaped off the chaise under a cloud of flying popcorn.

"Everett, did you see that?"

He bolted up. "See what?"

"Something ran across the room!"

"What do you mean something ran across the room?"

"Look, Everett, I don't know what it was. Just turn on the lights."

By now, I was standing on the chaise, fearfully eyeing the floor. Everett got up and turned on the light.

"Where did you see it?"

"It ran toward the drapes."

He opened them and carefully looked around.

"Babe, there's nothing here."

"I'm telling you I saw something! I was watching the movie, and something darted across the room."

Everett started laughing. "Michelle, you scared the hell out of me. It was a scene from the movie. Didn't you see the woman walk into the kitchen? As soon as she turned on the light, a rat darted from beneath the kitchen table and ran toward her!"

OMG! Had I been so wrapped up in my fantasy about Everett that I thought a rat had scurried across the room? Girl, get it together! You just tossed popcorn everywhere!

I was still standing on the chaise and Everett approached me with a bemused expression.

"It's okay, babe," he soothed. "I know you didn't mean to redecorate the family room with popcorn. It's obvious your mind was on something else."

I felt the heat rise on my cheeks.

"Everett, I'm so embarrassed! I'll clean it up."

"Don't be." He gently pulled me onto the chaise. "I think we've seen enough of the movie."

He dimmed the lights and snuggled beside me. He gazed into my eyes for a few moments.

"Michelle, we've been together for a few months, and I'm sure you also feel that our time together has been amazing."

"Yes, it has."

"You know," he murmured, "we truly are connected. As we lay together, I started imagining how it would be to make passionate love to you. By your actions this evening, I'm guessing you were thinking the same. Am I right?"

Tingling warmth suffused my body. "I feel the same."

Everett pulled me close, cupped my chin, and kissed me. This time, I didn't hold back. I kissed him just as passionately as he kissed me.

"Babe, is it okay if I touch you?"

"Yes! Please, yes!"

He unbuttoned my pants and slowly pulled them down. My heart was thundering in my chest. I felt like the air had been sucked from my lungs.

"Babe, are you okay?"

I whispered, "Yes, I'm good."

"You sure you want to take it further?"

"I'm sure."

My body's response was the signal Everett needed to know I was ready, and we made love on the chaise lounge. As our bodies moved in effortless synchronicity, it felt almost like an out-of-body experience. Everything far exceeded what I imagined. With every kiss, Everett breathed life into my soul. He was an unselfish lover and patiently explored my body with his hands and provided pleasure that satisfied us both. Eyes closed, savoring the intensity of feeling him deep inside of me, I had to remind myself to breathe as I lay beneath his strong body.

"Open your eyes," he whispered. "I want you to see me, and I want to see the look in your eyes when you have an orgasm."

That evening we became one mind, one body.

After that, our friendship soared to a new level. Everett adored me, and I felt the same. My professional and personal lives were great, and I finally had the man of my dreams. He brought joy back into my life and made me feel valued and appreciated. When it came to us, our time was precious to him, and he wouldn't allow his friends or family to interrupt. He always put us first. Or so I thought.

On one of the nights when I stayed at his house, Everett and I had just made love and were in bed having a pleasant conversation. Suddenly, his mood abruptly changed, and he appeared deep in thought.

"Are you okay?" I asked, wondering if I'd done something wrong.

"Yes, I'm good."

"Are you sure?"

"Babe… I have to tell you that you're not the only woman in my life."

Dumbstruck, I struggled to process what he said. We were together most of the time. How did he find the time to be with someone else? My mind swirled. Damn, did I just get played? Give up the coochie, and the MF comes clean!

I lay there replaying his words and silently looked at

him. Girl, say something! The situation had become so surreal I wondered if I was dreaming. Did I know Everett or only the persona he presented? The more I thought about it, the more I realized I saw what I wanted to see. I assumed he was my man, but he never asked me to be his girlfriend.

Do I stay and enjoy him or just cut it off? Do I ask the questions I should have before I slept with him? Do I want to be that insecure, jealous woman filled with questions? I was fully conscious of my actions and decided not to get angry, so I stayed. I could almost hear Jennifer scolding me. But was I stupid for staying?

Some women might say I was foolish for staying, but how many times have women stayed or knew someone who stayed and accepted the man's explanations? Women stayed, and if the sex was spectacular, for damn sure, they were going to think twice, as love or lust was as powerful as any drug.

I wanted Mr. Right, and I got him! So, I chose to ignore what he confessed. The sex was incredible, and our reciprocal candor opened the door for easy communication. There was little to no drama, and laughter always filled the room.

I accepted that Everett wasn't the man I'd marry. He'd just be my Mr. Right for now. I rose, looked him squarely in the eyes, and said, "Just do me a favor and change the sheets." Then I thought, Who am I trying to impress by saying something that stupid? I thought I was trying to be strong, but I felt used and betrayed. I couldn't blame Everett for pulling down my pants. He asked, and I agreed.

Chapter Nine

Everett and I continued to see each other regularly, and I didn't pressure him for a commitment. I let him see that I was confident and secure, with or without him. Then, eight months into our relationship, he did something I didn't expect. Although we worked in the same building, we didn't spend every waking minute together. Our work lives were completely separate from our personal lives. I never mixed the two anyway, and people could think what they wanted. Occasionally, we met for lunch or took a short walk.

One afternoon, I was at my desk when I received an instant message from the company receptionist, Mrs. Rize, notifying me that I had a package. I locked my office and went to the front desk. On the way, I noticed a few of my co-workers in the hallway. I politely greeted them and hurried into the empty elevator before anyone could join me. I wasn't in the mood for mindless office conversation and just wanted to get to the ground floor. When I stepped out, I heard Mrs. Rize speaking on the phone. She was overdressed as usual and wearing a cloying floral perfume. She nodded as I approached.

"Ms. Davis, a package came for you today. I'll get it from the mailroom."

"Thanks," I said, trying not to inhale the fragrance too deeply.

A few minutes later, she returned with a medium-sized blue box decorated with orange ribbons and an elaborate bow. By her curious expression and since she was strictly business, I knew she was wondering who sent Ms. Busy Bee, the name some in the office called me, a personal gift.

"Looks so lovely," she said with a tone that begged for more details.

"Thank you, Mrs. Rize," I said, taking the box and feeling her eyes on me as I walked away.

When I returned to my office, I examined the box and noticed it was from a local bakery. I wondered who sent it because I never received personal mail or deliveries at work. I opened the box, and inside was a smaller white box with a note that read, A little treat before dinner. Won't spoil your appetite. Dinner tonight at seven. Love, Everett. Inside the box was a large white cupcake layered with cream cheese and raspberry frosting topped with a single raspberry. The cupcake sat on a clear plate inside a circle of raspberries and smelled absolutely divine.

I was so overwhelmed by Everett's generosity that tears of joy flooded my eyes. I wondered why he'd send me a gift at work after all this time. Was it his way of making up for sleeping with two women? I didn't know how to respond. Call or text? I was determined to remain in control of this scenario. I certainly didn't want him to hear the happiness in my voice, so I texted him. Hi, Everett. Just got the gift. It truly made my day. Looking forward to dinner. Thank you. kiss emoji.

Unable to resist the cupcake any longer, I retrieved a plastic fork from my desk and took a generous bite. The exquisite combination of sweet, creamy, and tart flavors exploded in my mouth. It was so delicious that I wasted no time devouring the succulent treat. I had to give Everett credit for this delightful surprise.

I'd barely finished the cupcake when my phone started ringing, and emails started piling up in my inbox. Add some last-minute meetings and people stopping by my office, I prayed for the day to end. When I finally left, I was mentally exhausted.

As I passed the reception area, Mrs. Rize called out, "So what was in the box, Ms. Davis?"

I bit my tongue. What damn business was it of hers to call me out in front of others? I'd been with the company for several years. She knew I was very private and never discussed my personal life on the job.

Displaying my irritation, I said tartly, "It was a cupcake, Mrs. Rize. A very delicious one."

"Secret admirer?" she asked.

I continued walking toward the exit without making eye contact. "Have a good evening, Mrs. Rize."

As I walked toward the parking garage, I saw Mr. Shelton walking in my direction.

"Hi, Mr. Shelton. How was your day?"

"Busy as usual. Just glad to be off of work."

"Me too. I'm exhausted!"

"I've noticed you and Everett leaving the building together," he said.

What was it about my personal life tonight that everyone needed to comment on?

"Mr. Shelton, you need to stop. Everett and I are just friends."

He shook his head with a slight smile, "If you say so, Ms. Davis."

"I do say so. Have a good evening Mr. Shelton. See you tomorrow."

"You too, Ms. Davis."

When I got to my car, I had to calm down. Waiting to exit the garage behind the other cars, I turned up the music and relaxed to the sound of ocean waves. I took a few deep breaths. I really just wanted to go home and smoke a joint, but I had a dinner date with Everett.

When I finally got home, I hurried because I only had an hour to get ready. I freshened up and changed into a pair of high-waisted ripped jeans and a white-laced cami top. Glancing longingly at the joint on my nightstand, I was tempted to take a hit but knew if I did, I wasn't going anywhere. Before heading out the door, I grabbed my boho floral cardigan and put on my blue sneakers.

As I drove, I wondered why Everett had sent me that delicious cupcake. Was it part of a plan? What was he up to? Curious to find out, I sped up. When I got to his place, I parked in the driveway and used the keypad entry to access the garage doorway.

As I stepped through the door, I called out, "Hi, babe, I'm here."

"Cool! Come on up."

Walking up the stairs, I met a delicious aroma. "My God!" I exclaimed. "That smells incredible. What are you cooking?"

"Babe, tonight we're having seafood gumbo with turkey sausage, crab, and shrimp over jasmine rice, a side salad, and a chilled bottle of white wine."

"Looks like I'm being spoiled today!" I said with a smile. "Can I at least help you with dinner?"

"Chef works alone," he said. "But you can get the wine from the bar downstairs."

"I can do that. Be right back."

When I stepped into Everett's playroom, the memories of our evening playing pool swirled in my mind. I ran my hand along the side rail of the pool table and savored the softness of the red felt lining. Suddenly, I envisioned myself naked on the table while Everett explored my body. I shivered from arousal and leaned against the table to support myself. Lost in the memory of that night, I didn't hear Everett come into the room.

"Thought you got lost, babe," he said with a smile.

Startled, I struggled to compose myself.

"No," I said, pretending to look around the room. "I was just remembering what fun we had during our game."

Everett looked at me for a moment. He silently approached, gently sat me on the pool table, and stood between my thighs. I almost fainted from his touch. Damn, was this really happening? Everett's eyes shone with desire. He spread my legs and trailed his fingers along my inner thighs.

"I think we should indulge in an appetizer, don't you?"

My heart thudded so loudly that I barely heard his words.

Everett slowly lifted my cami top and teased the lace of my bra before unhooking it. My throbbing sweet spot painfully ached, and the sound of my breathing filled the room. Everett cupped my breasts and devoured each one. Each flick of his tongue left a sizzling trail on my skin.

"Everett… I can't … if you don't stop …"

"If I don't stop, what?" he whispered.

"I'm so hungry …" I murmured.

"Don't worry about dinner, babe. Got that under control."

Everett gathered me in his arms and laid me on the carpet. As he removed my clothes, every cell of my body vibrated from his touch. For a moment, he gazed at me as though admiring a painting in a museum. Smiling softly, he trailed his hands along my body until they teased my sweet spot.

I jerked and cried out, the last of my reserve fading away as I surrendered him. Pausing only to strip off his clothing, we continued our sensual dance.

Afterward, we lay entwined until we recovered. My skin resonated with his cologne and fueled my desire yet again. I wanted more. I just couldn't get enough of him.

"Did I satisfy your craving?" Everett whispered in my ear.

I smiled. He already knew me so well.

"Maybe we should have our dinner before I get another one," I said.

He laughed and got up. Walking naked to the bar, he retrieved the wine from the cooler.

"Really?" I said, slipping on my clothes.

He took a moment to dress and guided me back to the kitchen.

"Now that we've had dessert have a seat while Chef Everett finishes preparing his culinary masterpiece!"

I sat at a beautifully set table. Watching Everett cook

was entertaining and revealed his admirable skill as a chef. I smiled inwardly, knowing there'd be no fast-food excuses in this household.

"I have to thank you again for that fantastic cupcake," I said. "I devoured it like I hadn't seen food in days."

Everett laughed. "I love a woman with a good appetite!"

"And I love a man that knows how to satisfy a woman with a good appetite."

We both laughed. Everett walked to the fridge and showed me a box of mini chocolate cupcakes topped with frosting and plump strawberries. I eyed the miniature masterpieces.

"Now you're spoiling me," I said. "First, I get dessert before dinner, a personal chef for the evening, and now, more dessert!"

Everett grinned. "Chef Everett always aims to please!"

After Everett finished preparing dinner, he served the gumbo and poured two glasses of white wine.

"Hungry?"

"Starving!" I confirmed. "I was almost tempted to eat another cupcake."

"I admire your self-control when it comes to food, but where's your self-control when it comes to me?"

I laughed. "Babe, you're my favorite flavor, but dinner smells extremely appetizing right now!"

Everett sat down next to me at the table. "Of course!" he said, "But before we eat, I have to tell you something."

My heart almost jumped into my throat. Oh God, what now? He already dropped a bomb on me with the other woman issue. I tried to steady my nerves.

"What is it?"

"I've given our relationship much thought. We've been together for eleven months, and I couldn't be happier. How do you feel about being my girlfriend?"

For a moment, all I could do was stare at him. My mind raced. Damn, why now? I wondered if the other woman Everett had supposedly been seeing kicked his ass to the curb, and I'd become his fallback chick. But I wasn't seeing anyone else, and I truly enjoyed being with him, no matter how unusual our relationship was.

Everett watched me carefully.

"Well, Michelle, what do you think?"

I took a breath and composed myself.

"Everett, I have to be honest. When you told me you were involved with another woman, it was a terrible shock. I pretended it didn't bother me, but it did. I've been down this road before, and I need the person in my life to be honest with me."

Everett sat down and clasped my hands.

"Michelle, I understand, and for that, I apologize. I truly enjoy being with you and want to see where this relationship goes. If your answer is yes, then I'd like you to move in with me and eventually become Mrs. Michelle James." Everett reached into his pocket and pulled out a small black velvet box. He looked me in the eyes and opened the box. I was pleasantly surprised when I saw the Le Vian Chocolate Diamond with layers of chocolate and nude diamonds. I wondered if this was a girlfriend ring or an engagement ring. "Michelle, for now, would you accept my proposal to be my girlfriend?" Everett asked.

Warmth rushed through my body. I felt excited but wary and didn't want to make the mistake of rushing things.

"Everett, the ring is absolutely beautiful. I'd love to be your girlfriend and, one day, your wife, but moving in will have to wait. I feel strongly that we should continue as we are and get to know each other better. We can revisit moving in another time."

Everett kissed my hand and slipped the ring on my left hand's ring finger. "Babe, I understand and respect your decision. Just know the door's always open to you. Now, let's enjoy our meal."

I felt it was important not to give up my home, considering Everett freely admitted that he'd been seeing another woman. Moving in with him at that time would have been an enormous mistake. Honestly, I didn't care if he understood or not. This time, I'd do what was best for me. I was tired of trying to please men when they only considered me a temporary amusement.

As time passed, relentlessly and lovingly, Everett asked once a month if I'd given his request any consideration. After four months, I agreed because he proved to be trustworthy, and most days after work, I went directly to his place. I even left clothes there. This way, I didn't have to wake up early to go home and dress for work, and he did the same when he stayed at my house. It just made sense. Before I moved in with Everett, I reminded him of the conversation we had about honesty. He promised that no matter what was going on in his life, he'd honor my request for transparency. Before I sold my home and moved in with him, I called my mom to give her the news.

"Hi, Mom," I said.

"Hi, sweetie. How are you?"

"I'm good."

"What's going on?"

Excitedly, I said, "Well, I have some news for you. I decided to sell my house and move in with Everett."

For a moment, I heard only silence.

"Michelle, are you serious? You just met the man. Take a moment to think about what you're committing to. Don't you think you're rushing things?"

I tried to contain my irritation.

"Mom, Everett and I have been together for over a year; it's not like I just met him. So far, our relationship is going well. I'm not a child. I'm a grown woman. I know what I'm doing. You don't have to worry."

"I know you are, sweetie, but I feel strongly that you should wait to get married. I don't think you should sell your house. Why don't you just rent it?"

"Mom, I don't want the headache of renting. I'm busy enough as it is, and having to oversee a rental is more than I can or want to handle. I've made my decision. As I said, I know what I'm doing."

"Sweetie, I understand, but have you considered hiring a property management company to oversee the property? You worked hard and sacrificed to buy your home. This is your investment. Why not rent it out and make a profit?"

"Mom, if I hire a management company, and they fail to vet the tenants thoroughly, and my home is destroyed, the repair costs come out of my pocket. Yes, there are pros and cons, but I feel there are more cons than pros. But if this gets you off my back, I'll definitely think about it!"

Mom's pained sigh echoed in my ear. I could almost see her disapproving expression. I knew my comment upset her. I did my best not to disrespect her, but she just refused to listen. I thought my sister was bad, but sometimes with Mom, it was often her way or the highway. I heard her exhale, and I braced myself for what she'd say.

"Michelle, can I get you to pause for a minute? Look at what happened when Chase moved in with you. You were heartbroken and cried for months when he called off the wedding and left. If I were you, I'd hold onto your house just in case things don't work out. By the way, have you spoken with your sister about your decision to move in with Everett?"

Here we go again. Was it possible to have a conversation that didn't involve the family? I felt the heat rise to my face.

Before I realized it, I yelled, "No! I haven't! You know how Cheri is. If I don't take her advice, she gets upset and gives me a long lecture. I love her, but I'm just not in the mood to hear how she thinks I should run my life." I paused. "Mom, why don't you think my relationship with Everett will work out?"

"I'm not saying it won't, Michelle. You have to be practical and have a backup plan! But I see you're determined. I'll support your decision even though I think you're making a mistake. But it's your life, not mine, and you know I only want the best for my baby girl."

So now, she wants to call me her baby girl to make me feel bad for not listening or taking her guidance.

"Thanks, Mom. I know you don't understand, but I truly appreciate your support. Please forgive my rudeness; I didn't mean to be disrespectful. Can we just table this conversation for now?"

"Sure, Michelle."

"We'll talk later. I love you."

"Love you too. Bye."

I wasn't surprised that Mom wasn't happy with my decision, but I was in love, and the thought of coming home to Everett every day filled my heart with joy. Sometimes, it was easy for a woman to judge another woman's actions when love captured her heart. While women realized falling in love was a personal journey and different for every woman, women tended to follow their hearts instead of their heads. When it came to Everett, I didn't distort reality. To protect my heart, I didn't fantasize about becoming his wife. I just loved him the way I wanted to be loved.

Chapter Ten

The move into Everett's home was seamless, considering we'd been practically living together. After I sold my house, and due to limited space in Everett's home, I put most of my furnishings in storage. He wanted me to feel comfortable, so he cleared half of his large walk-in closet for me and turned one of the bedrooms into my personal space. When it came to housework and maintenance, we functioned in harmony, but he did most of the cooking. I was in a thriving relationship but now struggled because I insisted that we remain open and honest.

In most areas of my life, I was forthright with Everett. However, I never revealed my addiction to change. Ten months after the move, I was presented with a job opportunity in a different state. I certainly wasn't about to decline an opportunity to advance my career, but I hesitated to tell Everett for fear of disappointing him. He apologized for sleeping with another woman and settled down with me, but the thought of a new adventure called me like a siren's song.

The thrill of the unknown, searching for a new home, and discovering new things was as alluring as an orgasm. It wasn't an area in my life I was prepared to surrender. I knew I eventually had to tell Everett about the job opportunity, so I chose sooner. I'd barely picked up the phone to call him when my sister, Cheri, called.

"Hey, sis, what's up?" I asked.

"Not much. Just checking in on you. How are things with Everett, and how is this living together working out for you?"

If I could have reached through the phone, I would have smacked her judgmental face. Now, don't misunderstand. I loved my big sister, and if anyone disrespected her, I wouldn't hesitate to kick their ass. But she always had my parents' approval for doing what was right, whatever right was.

"It's actually working out great, Cheri."

I wanted to tell her about the job opportunity but feared she'd ask questions I wasn't prepared to answer.

"That's good to hear," she replied. "You know, more than anything, I want you to be happy, and if there ever comes a time when you're not, please don't hesitate to call me."

"Thanks. If that day ever comes, I'll call you. Look, I hate to cut the conversation short, but I was about to call Everett when you buzzed."

"No problem. We can chat later. Love you."

"Love you too. Bye for now."

As I gripped my phone, a wave of nausea overwhelmed me. I knew it was just anxiety, but I couldn't control my shaking hands. With a thudding heart, I tapped out Everett's number. One ring, two rings, three rings, four rings. Just as I was about to breathe a sigh of relief, he answered.

"Hey, babe, what's up?"

"Not much other than work. I was calling to see if you want to meet for lunch at 11:30."

"Babe, I'd love to," he sighed, "but I have a meeting then and am going to lunch afterward, so I'll be staying late at the office."

"Okay, no worries. See you at home tonight. I love you."

"What did you just say?" he asked quickly.

"I said, no worries, see you at home tonight."

"No. What did you say after that?"

I paused and smiled. "I said I love you."

"Oh, my pretty lady loves her man. Babe, I love you too. Looking forward to seeing you this evening."

Damn! I wanted to tell him, but he sounded so upbeat that I didn't have the nerve to spoil the mood. When I drove home after work, I was relieved because Everett wouldn't be home for a few hours, but my anxiety was now at hurricane level. I had to calm down and appear cool and collected. If I looked like a nervous wreck, the situation could become disastrous, so I took a few drags of my joint and relaxed on the bed. Feeling lightheaded from the joint, I heard Everett calling my name.

"Hey, babe, wake up."

Rubbing my eyes, I gazed up at Everett standing over the bed.

"Hey, luv. I must have drifted off."

"I can see that. You're still wearing your shoes. Good thing I picked up some dinner."

Trying to focus, I said, "That was sweet of you. Let's eat. I'm starving."

"No rush," he said, kissing me. "Let me get changed. It's been a long day."

I savored the taste of his lips before I got up.

"Babe," I uttered, "I'm going downstairs."

"Okay. Be down in a minute."

A delicious aroma drew me to the kitchen. I peeked into two pizza boxes. One was veggie for me, and the other was a meat-lovers for Everett. Although I was hungry, my stomach roiled from anxiety. How would I start the conversation? Talking was never an issue, but Everett and I were in a good place, and I feared my news would jeopardize our relationship. As I stood debating, he walked in.

"Babe, it's great to be home. Thought the day would never end." He dropped into the nearby chair. "I'm famished. That meeting dragged on forever, so I never had lunch."

"Why don't you sit down?" I stated. "Feel like wine or a beer?"

"Thanks, babe. A beer would be lovely."

I got two Coronas from the fridge, grabbed the pizzas, and sat next to him.

"Thanks again for picking up dinner," I said. "Work was crazy today too, and I was wiped out when I got home."

For a few minutes, we ate silently. Everett paused to take a sip of his beer and looked at me.

"What's going on at work that's keeping you so busy?"

"The mentoring program," I said with a sigh. "Not enough mentors."

"Well, I'm sure my babe can handle it."

"Yeah. I'll figure something out." I took a bite of pizza.

"Anything else going on? You look a little preoccupied."

"Well, mostly work, and ..."

"And what?"

"Well, a recruiter from JCI Enterprise, Inc, contacted me. They offered me a managerial position in their Chicago corporate office, in their Acquisitions Department, and the company offers upward mobility, therefore, it's a fantastic opportunity."

My heart sank when I saw the surprise in his eyes. He watched me for a few moments before responding.

Everett stopped chewing. "I really don't know how to respond." He paused. "Were you looking for another job?"

"No. My resume is posted on my LinkedIn profile."

"Are you accepting the offer?"

"Yeah, I think so. I know we just took a major step in our relationship, but this is a once-in-a-lifetime opportunity. My career is on a fast track, and I'll have my own division."

Everett leaned back in his chair. "I understand, but don't you think we should discuss this before you make a life-changing decision?"

"Of course, your opinion matters, and I don't want my decision to jeopardize our relationship."

"Do you have a start date?"

"Yes, in three months."

"Well, it seems you've already made your decision," he said, rolling his eyes.

"Yes, I have."

I sensed Everett's disappointment. Perhaps I should have told him sooner, but I didn't want to deal with potential conflict sooner than necessary.

He reached for my hand. "Michelle, you know I don't want to hold you back, but I want you here. We're in a good space. Why put distance between us now?"

"Everett, Chicago is just a four-hour drive. We could see each other every weekend."

"I see you've given this some thought. Why don't we do this? Take the job for a year, and if distance starts to affect our relationship, then you'll relocate back here. If you agree, then I'll support your decision."

I hugged him with a mixture of relief and gratitude.

"Yes! That's fine. I was so nervous about telling you. I thought you wouldn't understand."

"Babe, I know you're career driven. I knew that before you moved in, and I'm not going to be selfish even though I want you here with me. Don't worry. We'll be just fine. Now, let's finish our dinner and enjoy each other's company."

I was pleasantly surprised that Everett understood and supported my decision to accept the job in Chicago. He wasn't forcing us into a long-distance relationship. I was, which meant I'd have to make a concerted effort to see him. Most long-distance relationships failed, but Everett and I were determined to make it work. We knew it would be challenging but felt our love could stand the test. It was the heart of our relationship, and the flame that drew us together was burning hot.

To ensure there was no disconnect in our relationship, we'd call each other daily and see each other at weekends. Before I left, Everett took me to the Mediterranean restaurant where we had our first date, and afterward, we went dancing. The nightclub was lively, and the music energized us the moment we walked inside. We didn't bother looking for a place to sit but went directly to the dance floor and grooved to the beat of old-school R&B music. Our eyes reflected our feelings without words, so we danced and held each other close.

The evening was undoubtedly one of the happiest moments of my life. It was around midnight when we returned home. Still high from dancing, we decided to sit on the deck. Everett grabbed two Corona beers from the fridge, and I got the weed. It was a chilly evening but not cold, so we cuddled together in a blanket with our beers and weed and listened to the soothing stillness of the night. I gazed at the vista of glittering stars. They twinkled like celestial Morse Code as if sending the message, It's okay to accept change. Just like the constellations changed positions over time, people did the same. Otherwise, we become stagnant.

Snuggled beside Everett, I couldn't think of a place I'd rather be. I looked into his eyes and wondered if I really needed more in my life. Couldn't I just be content with the job I had? But I was born with a gypsy spirit, and change had become my drug of choice. It was an addiction I had struggled with most of my life; I was always searching for something bigger and better. No matter how often I told myself that enough was enough, I wanted more. When the time came for a change, I moved on without a second thought and with no concern for anyone else's input, as addicts do. One more hit was what we told ourselves. Because I had reservations, I was glad I wasn't moving for a few months.

During that time, I decided to talk to Jennifer about it. I told her I was struggling with my decision to move but felt if I didn't accept this opportunity and the relationship failed, I'd be left with painful regrets. Her advice was simply to follow my heart and not worry about the what-ifs. If it was meant to be, it would happen. Jennifer had always been more than my best friend, and she always knew about my addiction to change. For as long as I could remember, she was always my anchor in stormy seas and that voice of reason I could rely on. She listened and advised me but never attempted to pressure me into taking her advice.

She simply said, "Just do you. If you fail, then you have only yourself to blame."

~

After speaking with Jennifer, I knew I had to make the inevitable call to my mom. I dreaded telling her because the first words out of her mouth would be, "Then why in the hell did you move in with Everett if you were looking for a job?" But I'd be leaving soon, and if I didn't tell her, she'd feel like I was hiding an important part of my life from her. Mom was very opinionated. If it wasn't her way, it was the wrong way. No matter what I achieved or accomplished, it was never enough.

Cheri was 36 and owned and operated two daycare centers. My brother Aaron, 39, was a prominent data engineer. Both were married with children. Then there was me, 34, the youngest, with a great job, no husband, no children, and a track record of failed relationships. Instead of telling my mom, I decided to call my dad. Dad was quiet, easy-going, a hard worker, and well-read. His main goal in life was to financially provide for his family. With him, no subject was off-limits. I knew he'd listen without overreacting, so I called him.

"Hi, Sunshine! I was just thinking about you. How are you doing? How are things with Everett?"

Hearing my dad's voice instantly comforted me. He called me Sunshine because as a child, I was always cheerful even when the weather was gloomy, and my smile could light up a room.

"I'm good, Dad. And things with Everett are even better."

"That's wonderful to hear. Your mom wasn't happy with your decision to shack up, and she lets me know that every day. I keep telling her that you're a grown woman, and you're going to do whatever you want to do."

"Which is why I'm calling you. JCI Enterprise made me an offer to work at their Chicago corporate office, in their Acquisitions Department. Dad, an Acquisition manager position was made available to me. It's a great career move. I accepted the offer and will depart in a few months."

"That's wonderful news, sunshine! Have you told Mom?"

"Well, no. I was hoping you'd tell her. You know how she is. She wasn't happy with my decision to move in with Everett, and now I'm moving again. You can tell her, Dad. Just bring her to the phone."

He sighed. "Sunshine, that's not how we operate. You're an adult, so you'll have to call and tell her."

"But, Dad …"

"Don't play that with me, Michelle. You're going to call your mother after I hang up."

"Okay, Dad," I said resignedly.

"Talk with you later, sunshine."

"Bye, Dad. Love you. Please don't tell her I told you?"

"I won't. Just call her now."

Chapter Eleven

I woke up early Sunday morning to the sound of thunder and heavy rain. I had a slight headache, and the weight of telling my mom weighed heavily on my mind. I turned over and cuddled Everett as he slept soundly. I draped my arm over his waist and held him close. As we lay in bed, Everett woke up and said, "Good morning, babe."

"Good morning, luv, I hope I didn't wake you."

Everett turned towards me, and said, "Well, you did, but that's fine. What's on your mind? Are you unable to sleep?"

"Well, you know, I spoke with my dad yesterday, and he urged me to call my mom and tell her about the job." I briefly hesitated. "But...my mom has strong opinions, and there are times when I just wish she would listen to me and accept my decision, so I asked Dad to tell her."

"Babe, just call your mom. She'll understand. Stop worrying. It's all going to work in your favor.

"I know, it's just..."

"Babe, stop. It's going to be fine."

Everett always knew what to say or do to bring serenity into my life whenever he sensed that I was stressed. And, this rainy morning, he knew exactly what to do to ease my mind. He drew me in and kissed my neck before signaling for me to turn on my side. He then filled me with his morning splendor when I did. We then cuddled in bed, spoke, and enjoyed the sound of the rain. As I laid next to him, I thought about the conversation I had with Dad and was glad he wouldn't mention our conversation to Mom or the rest of the family. If my mom knew I told Dad before telling her, let's just say all hell would break loose.

After silently wrestling with the thought of calling my mom, I kissed Everett and got out of bed. I retrieved my phone and joint from the nightstand and went downstairs. I made a cup of green tea and lit my joint. After a couple of drags, I tapped out Mom's number.

"Hi, Mom."

"Hey, sweetie, how are you doing?"

"I'm great."

"That's good to hear."

Just rip off the bandage and tell her!

"Mom, I have some wonderful news. I received a job offer from JCI Enterprise to work at their corporate office in Chicago. I will oversee all intel acquisitions and have my own division."

"When did this happen, Michelle?" she asked sharply.

I tried not to be put off by her tone.

"About two weeks ago."

"Two weeks ago, and you're just now telling me?"

"Well, I wanted to weigh the pros and cons before announcing it."

If she knew I'd spoken with Dad, she'd have exploded. Even if she asked him if I'd told him, I knew he'd simply sidestep the question.

"I take it there were more pros than cons?"

"Yes, Mom. Quite a few. This is an amazing career move, and my salary will practically double."

"Really?" she said dryly. "What about Everett? How does he feel about all this? I don't understand why you'd move in with him if you were looking for a job. It doesn't make sense, Michelle."

I knew she'd say that. But what did I expect?

"I wasn't looking for a job. Their recruiter contacted me. My LinkedIn profile includes my resume. They obviously read it and decided I was a good fit for their company. As I said, Mom, it's a fantastic opportunity, and Everett's fine with my decision."

Her brief silence signaled her disapproval. I clearly saw her expression in my mind.

"I just hope you know what you're getting yourself into. Are you positive this is what you want to do?"

"Yes, Mom. I am."

"Okay," she sighed, "if that's what you want, I won't talk you out of going. When are you leaving?"

"In a couple of months."

"Do you think you can come home before moving to Chicago?"

"Not sure. Everything I took to Everett's house has to be packed and moved into my storage unit. The next two months will pass quickly. You know I'm not a last-minute person. If I have time, I'll definitely try to come home."

"Okay. It's been a while, and I'd love to see my baby girl."

"I know, Mom. I'll do my best. Chat later."

"Okay, luv, bye."

I sagged with relief. The conversation went better than expected, and I was glad it was finally over.

Over the next two months, Everett and I packed my belongings and moved the boxes to the storage unit. The plan was to have the boxes and my furniture in storage shipped after I found a place to live. I reached my final work week at Marcell Technologies. On my last day of work, I was stunned that my work team organized an office get-together and wished me success in my new job because most of my co-workers referred to me as Unsociable Michelle. However, my co-workers knew I was a team player, that I was open and considerate of their opinions, and that I'd gladly assist them whenever necessary.

They felt I was not sociable because I only attended mandatory office functions in eight years on the job, occasionally went to lunch with a few co-workers, and celebrated after hours with the same people. I maintained a no-nonsense work ethic, and being mission-focused allowed me to advance quickly on the job. I wasn't bothered by anyone's opinion of me. I was hired to do a job which I completed successfully.

My team presented me with a card containing money, a lovely bouquet of flowers, a cake, and refreshments. It was a kind gesture, and I appreciated their efforts. I said my goodbyes, turned in my office key, and left. I also wanted to say goodbye to Mr. Shelton. I walked to the security station, reliving fond memories of where I first met Everett, and saw Mr. Shelton warmly greeting everyone.

"Hi, Mr. Shelton. How's it going?"

He turned to me with a broad smile.

"So far, all is well. I hear it's your last day."

"Yes, it is."

"You're leaving us to join our competition?" he joked.

"Let's just say, a good job."

He shook my hand. "Ms. Davis, I wish you success. I'm glad I was able to introduce you to Everett. You seem very happy."

"We are, Mr. Shelton." I removed my badge and handed it to him. "I won't need this anymore."

"Thanks, Ms. Davis. You take care."

"I will. You do the same."

As I pulled out of the parking garage, I glanced in the rearview mirror to see the last eight years of my career fade into my past. It seemed surreal that it was over. Now I had only two weeks to prepare for the move. So much to do in a short amount of time. I pressed the voice command in my car and said, "Call Everett on cell."

"Hey, babe, what's up?" he asked, answering on the second ring.

"I've processed out of the job. You, okay?"

"Yeah, just busy. I've been tasked with a last-minute business trip to Washington, D.C."

"When and how long?"

"I leave in a couple of days."

"What? You've got to be kidding me! That's Sunday! You know I'm leaving in a couple of weeks."

"I know! I tried to get out of going, but the person assigned got sick, so now I'm stuck with it."

"Are you certain you can't get out of the trip?"

"No, I can't, babe. I'm sorry. I have to go. Talk later."

"Everett! Everett!"

Silence was all I heard as he hung up.

This couldn't be happening! Not now! I pushed the voice command again.

"Call Everett!"

The phone rang, but he didn't pick up. Oh, my God, I couldn't believe this! I was in such a good mood, and now this! Girl, you know if he could get out of going, he would.

Yeah, I'm talking to myself, but it's not doing a damn bit of good. Completely distracted, I drove through a red light on the way home. I was fortunate I didn't get a ticket or worse. Breathing a sigh of relief, I scolded myself. Girl, get yourself together before you have an accident!

When I got home fifteen minutes later, I went straight to the bedroom and took a few puffs of my joint. Once I calmed down, I changed into a white off-the-shoulder short mini-dress and went to the kitchen. I poured a glass of Moscato White wine and sat down at the table. I took a sip and said, "Alexa, play Chris Botti." By the time Everett got home, I was relaxed, and my emotional hurricane had dissipated. Noticing his tense expression, I decided to play it cool.

"You okay, babe? I tried calling you back."

"I know. I'm sorry I didn't pick up. Today has been the day from hell."

"What's going on?"

"Too many administrative changes and accompanying headaches. Look, let me get a hit of that joint."

"Better yet, babe, why don't you sit down? Let me help you relax." I lit the joint, took a hit, and exhaled. "Open your mouth," I said to Everett.

He opened his mouth and watched me curiously. I took a drag, pressed my lips to his, and blew smoke into his mouth. He inhaled deeply and released the smoke.

"Babe, one more time."

I repeated the process, but by now, Everett was smiling.

"Damn, Michelle! You definitely know how to make a man forget all his troubles. Pass me the joint." I handed it to him. He took two long drags and stood up. "Babe, I need a little something else from you."

"What, Everett?"

He smiled. Without a word, he bent me over the table, reached beneath my dress, and slowly pulled down my panties. Then he fucked me like there was no tomorrow. Yes, fuck, and it was fantastic!

~

Afterward, Everett and I lay intertwined in each other arms on the living room sectional. Now that he was relaxed, we calmly discussed his business trip and my move to Chicago.

"I understand that you're unable to get out of the trip. But can you meet me in Chicago over the weekend?"

Everett trailed his fingers across my face and teased my lips.

"I can't guarantee I can break away. The training is in D.C."

"Is this trip for training or a convention?"

"Training, and I'm scheduled to conduct part of the training. I train the latter of the first week and the beginning of the following week. I also have to review the material this weekend because I'm unprepared."

I tried to conceal my disappointment. "Babe, this isn't how I wanted to spend our last weekend together. We should be celebrating, not stressing."

"I know, babe. I promise I'll make it up to you. Why don't you help me pack? Then we'll have the rest of the weekend with each other."

"When's your flight on Sunday?" I asked.

"3:45 p.m."

"Okay. We'll have tonight and half of the day Saturday. I just need to review the training material Saturday evening."

Everett and I got up and began packing for his trip. I knew I needed to stay positive, but the little girl in me wanted to throw a tantrum and demand he tell his boss I was more important than this business trip. However, I realized that if I expressed my feelings, the mood would be spoiled. After all, I'd chosen to take the job in Chicago, and Everett had to consider his career as well. The sooner we finished packing, the sooner we could start enjoying our weekend.

"Done," Everett said, locking his luggage. "Why don't we grab a bite to eat?"

"Sounds good to me. Let me freshen up."

He laughed. "Guess I should do the same after what happened in the kitchen."

~

We drove to Hyde Park Square to our favorite sushi restaurant. We were pleasantly surprised it wasn't packed, given it was a Friday. The waitress immediately escorted us to a booth.

As we perused the menu, Everett paused, looked at me, and whispered, "Babe, I certainly enjoyed our session in the kitchen. Honestly, I'm looking forward to tonight."

"Same here, babe," I said, blushing. "We'd better order before our appetite shifts to something spicier."

Everett signaled the waitress. We ordered seaweed salads, shrimp tempura, a sushi and sashimi appetizer, crispy tofu, and garlic soft shell crab meal with two unsweetened iced teas. While we waited for our food, Everett leaned toward me.

"You know what I'd like you to do?" he whispered in my ear.

"What?"

"Go to the ladies' room, remove your panties, and bring them to me."

I initially thought he was joking until I saw the look in his eyes. "Everett, why are you being so freaky this evening?"

He didn't reply, but I noticed an odd expression I'd never seen before.

With a mischievous smile, I said, "I don't need to go to the ladies' room."

Ensuring that the tablecloth completely covered the table, I slowly reached under my dress, slipped off my panties, and placed them on his crotch. He grinned and inhaled deeply.

"Babe, let's get this to go," he said huskily.

When the waitress returned with our drinks, Everett asked, "Can we have our food to go?"

A few minutes later, our food arrived. Although it smelled amazing, we were hungry for something else. We drove to a secluded spot and fogged up the windows.

Our weekend turned out to be amazing. Everett spent quality time with me, and in between our lovemaking sessions, he had time to review his training material. We accepted that storms would occur and chose not to put energy into a situation out of our control. We simply showered each other with great conversation and love. We woke up early on Sunday and made love before enjoying breakfast. While Everett ensured he had everything for his trip, I cleaned the kitchen and tried to channel a more positive attitude. I wanted his departure to be pleasant. When the time came for us to leave, we loaded his luggage in the trunk, and I cheerfully drove to the airport.

On the way, I tuned the radio to Cool Jazz while Everett reviewed his flight itinerary and training schedule.

"Michelle, the next two weeks are going to be difficult. I haven't conducted training in quite a while. I should have scheduled an early flight. That way, I would have had more time to review the material and be better prepared."

"Babe, relax. You're excellent at your job. If your boss wasn't confident, you could handle the training, he wouldn't have asked. Stop worrying."

When we arrived at the airport, Everett turned down the music and said, "Babe, I'm going to miss you."

I reached for his hand and teased, "I know you will."

When we pulled up to the terminal, I helped Everett retrieve his luggage. I struggled to reign in my emotions. My eyes teared, and it was all I could do to stop myself from crying. Michelle, be strong! This isn't how you want to send him off.

When Everett closed the trunk, it sounded so final.

"Got everything?" I asked.

"Yes."

"Okay. You better get going. Don't want you to miss your flight."

Everett embraced me. I took a deep breath and relaxed in his arms. He cupped my chin, and we kissed passionately. As he walked toward the entrance, he turned and mouthed, "I love you. See you soon."

"I love you too," I said with a quavering voice. "See you soon!"

After he vanished into the terminal, I swallowed my tears and quickly drove off.

Chapter Twelve

The following day, I desperately needed a distraction from the sadness of Everett's departure and the silence reverberating from each room. So, I cleaned the entire house and started packing for my move to Chicago on Friday. By Thursday evening, I was fully packed, so I placed my luggage in the trunk of the car. Now that I was packed and didn't have the desire to cook, I ordered seared Ahi tuna with fried rice and fresh bean sprouts from the Cheesecake Factory along with a slice of banana cream cheesecake. When my food arrived, I poured a glass of Gray Goose vodka mixed with Sierra Mist, went into the den, and watched reruns of Girlfriends while I ate. After I finished my meal, I poured a second drink and prepared for bed. Before going to bed, I called Everett.

"Hi, babe, what's going on?"

"Not much. Just calling to confirm that you'll meet me in Chicago this weekend."

"Oh, I meant to inform you earlier that I can't make it."

"Are you sure? It's a nonstop flight, just two hours."

"I'm afraid I can't. I told you before I left that I'd be training at the end of this week and the beginning of next week. I need the weekend to prepare for the next week. I know you understand."

"Well, I have no choice but to understand."

"Come on, babe. Don't get upset."

"I'm not upset. I just hoped you could have come." I sighed and said, "Let's change the subject. How's the training?"

"It's going well. I was somewhat nervous, but I began to relax by the end of the first class."

"That's good to hear. I knew you could handle it."

"Yeah, you believed in me from the beginning. That's why I love you, and you know how to care for your man."

"Yes, I do, and don't you ever forget that." I yawned. "Well, I won't keep you on the phone much longer. I had a couple of vodka cocktails, and I'm tired."

"Oh, you're trying to turn up without me?" he replied with a laugh.

"No, I'm turning down without you." I giggled. "I'm getting ready to slide underneath the sheets and go to sleep."

"All right, babe. I miss you."

"Same here. Goodnight, luv."

The next morning, the shrill alarm on my cellphone jarred me awake. Was it seven already? I fumbled to switch it off and burrowed under the covers. I hadn't gotten enough sleep. I was disappointed that Everett couldn't meet me in Chicago and drinking too much vodka the night before caused me to spend half the night going to the bathroom.

I knew I needed to get out of bed because today was my travel day to Chicago, and I planned to be on the road by 8:30 a.m. Resignedly, I sat up and checked my phone. There was no message from Everett but one from Jennifer that read, Call me! I nestled against the pillows and tapped out her number.

"Hello."

"Hey, Jennifer. Got your message. What's up?" I yawned.

"Not much, just checking in on you. You all packed and ready to leave?"

"Yeah, I am."

"Hmmm… is that a little hesitation in your voice?"

"No … not really. Just tired and missing Everett."

"Isn't he coming to Chicago when he returns from his business trip?"

"That's the plan."

"So don't be moping in bed. Get up, fix your protein shake, and get ready to hit the road!"

"Okay, Mom, I will," I said with a laugh.

Jennifer chuckled. "Someone's got to be on your ass!"

"Yes, I can certainly count on you to keep me in line!"

"Just text me when you leave, and don't forget to share your location when you leave," Jennifer said.

"Will do. When I get settled, you've got to come for a visit."

"Girl, you know I'll be there. You and I are overdue for some quality girl time."

"Yes, we are. Once I get settled on the job, we need to start planning."

"Okay. Now, get your ass out of bed!"

"I'm getting up!" I laughed. "I'll text you before I get on the road. Love and miss you."

"See you soon. Safe travels."

After I hung up, I said a mental thank you to my best friend. She'd been with me through so many challenges in my life, and I was extremely grateful that she always had my back. As I completed my final morning routine and was ready to leave, I texted Everett. Hey Luv, I'm leaving, call me. I did a final walkthrough to ensure all the lights were off and all the doors were locked. Taking a last look at the house, I loaded the last of my things in the car and texted Jennifer. Hey Jennifer, I'm leaving, I'll text you when I arrive.

As I backed out of the garage, I lowered the window and took a moment to look at my neighborhood for the last time before I pulled out of the driveway. The skies were crystal blue, and birdsong filled the air. The perfection of the day felt like a good omen for my trip. Another chapter of my life was about to close. Excited and a little anxious about the next chapter, I wondered what it would bring. As I drove slowly down the street, I glanced into the rearview mirror and saw many memories of my life retreat into the past.

Before I got on the road, I stopped at a Speedway Gas Station and filled up my car. As I finished filling up, I remembered the water bottles I'd left on the kitchen counter, so I bought some from the store. Back on the road, I selected The Pulse station on SiriusXM and proceeded to I-74W for the five-hour drive to Chicago. I turned up the music, set the cruise control to 70 mph, and settled in for the drive. My goal was to stop halfway at Love Travel and Truck Stop to gas up, warm up my food, and get to Chicago before 6:00 p.m. so I could check in with the property manager of the apartment building where I'd be staying.

After an hour of driving, my phone chirped. On the stereo panel, I noticed a message from Everett, "Call me when you arrive. Love you." Puzzled, I wondered why he didn't just call. It would have been nice to talk to him. Not wanting to spoil the mood, I focused on the drive. Although the drive was monotonous, it was quite enjoyable because I had uninterrupted time to embrace my thoughts. As memories played through my mind, I recalled the sadness and heartbreak of my failed relationships. Yet the loneliness that had often been my enemy also provided an opportunity for reflection and analysis. It taught me to pursue what brought me joy, and my victory was embarking on a journey unique to me. Whether I failed or succeeded would be solely due to my actions and no one else's.

～

Three hours into the drive, I stopped for lunch. The Love Travel Stop was packed with travelers and truckers, and the lines at the gas pumps were backed up. I decided to park and headed to the ladies' room. The line there was just as long. From the sound of screaming kids and the look of exhausted mothers, it had been a long drive for everyone.

When I finished, I got into another line behind truckers heating up their food. Fifteen minutes later, feeling frustrated, I finally returned to my car with my warm food. I didn't want to wait around, so I got in the gas pump line. By the time I reached the pump, I'd eaten most of my lunch.

Still unsettled by the crowds and chaos, I parked in a quiet spot to finish my lunch and calm down before continuing the trip. I thought about Everett's message, and the more I mulled over it, the more irritated I became. Was he so busy that he couldn't take a minute to call me? The question bothered me so much that I decided to call him. After several rings, he finally picked up.

"Hey Michelle, what's going on?"

"What's going on? You know I'm driving to Chicago today."

"Yeah, yeah, I know. That's why I texted you this morning."

"Why didn't you just call me?"

"I thought you'd be too busy getting ready and would call once you were on the road."

"Well, talk about a slight miscommunication!"

"How's the drive so far?" he asked, ignoring my comment.

"It's been great. Just stopped for a break. I have a couple of hours left to go."

"Okay, I won't keep you."

My instincts started fluttering. Something about Everett's tone was too matter-of-fact. I could have been a stranger for all the emotion he showed.

"No time to talk?" I asked somewhat tartly.

"I do, Michelle. But I think you should get back on the road. Just text or call when you get there. I'm tired and was about to take a nap."

"It's past noon there. Why are you so tired? Did you go out last night after we spoke?"

"No! I just didn't get enough sleep last night. I came back to my room for a quick nap. Is that all right with you?"

"Okay, Everett, whatever. I'll call you when I arrive."

"Sure, Michelle. Talk later."

I hung up, fuming. It was difficult not to overreact as my female instincts were sounding a tsunami alert. No affection or emotion, and I seemed to have devolved from "Babe" to "Michelle." I pulled onto the I-74W ramp, turned up the music to calm myself and purge the negative conversation from my mind. I wasn't about to let Everett ruin my day.

~

I arrived in Chicago around 4:30ish on Friday, and bumper-to-bumper traffic greeted me. This wasn't my first time in Chicago, so I knew what to expect. The traffic was irritating because the drivers were in a constant rush and had no clue about road courtesy. With horns blowing, cars cutting each other off, and a roadside accident, I took my time driving to the corporate housing JCI Enterprise arranged.

My apartment was located at Divine Lakeshore Apartments about nine minutes from JCI's building in downtown Chicago. In the 46-story building, my apartment was located on the 20th floor. The building had the added security of a 24-hour doorman, private resident parking, and offered excellent amenities, such as the fitness center with a yoga studio, dry cleaning service, and a swimming pool. I checked in with the property manager and received the move-in checklist and the keys.

I was more than blown away when I opened the door to my apartment. I placed my backpack on the floor. On the kitchen counter stood a case of water and a beautiful welcome basket filled with assorted tea, coffee, fruit, cheese, crackers, and sparkling apple cider. Then I noticed the door to the balcony. Stepping outside, I took in the view, and my mouth dropped. The apartment overlooked the Chicago River and offered a spectacular view of the city. For several minutes, all I could do was stare.

"Hello, Chicago," I whispered.

I went back inside with the move-in checklist in my hand to complete my tour of the apartment. The sunlit living room was dominated by a bold aqua leather sectional that sat beautifully on gleaming hardwood floors. The wall-mounted flatscreen TV was precisely angled to be viewed from anywhere in the room. In addition to a fully equipped kitchen with a glass dining table and two aqua leather chairs, there was also an open breakfast nook just off the living room with a trio of silver metal barstools with soft blue cushions.

Down the hall from the kitchen and next to the guest bathroom, an apartment-size washer and dryer were neatly tucked behind a single white door. The two bedrooms were minimally furnished with king-size beds, two nightstands, lamps, large dressers, and a blue and orange abstract canvas picture above each bed. The bathroom was a clean white with aqua vanities. This stunning apartment was my home for approximately six months or less. Overwhelmed with joy, I sat on the sectional and called Everett.

"Hi, babe, I just got here. You should see my apartment! It's absolutely stunning. And the view overlooking the river is incredible!"

Everett laughed. "Whoa! Slow down! I take it the drive went well?"

I forced myself to slow down. "Yes, I enjoyed it. There's nothing like a road trip to clear your mind."

"Good. And we've clearly determined that you love your place!"

"I'll send you some pictures. I didn't expect it to be so gorgeous. The company even gave me a wonderful gift basket. I feel so spoiled!"

"Babe, you should hear the joy in your voice. I'm so happy everything's worked out well so far."

"No complaints," I said, noting his warmer tone.

"What are your plans for the rest of the day?"

"I'm going to unpack and take a breather. Later, if it's not too late, I'll check out the neighborhood. I still have a week left of my vacation. What are your plans?"

"Tonight, I'm getting together with some instructors for dinner and maybe drinks at a bar afterward. Now that you're there, I'll look at visiting after you settle in at your job. I've got one more week here, so I'll book a flight when I return home."

"That sounds wonderful, Everett. Just understand, I can't take additional time off."

"I understand. I miss you, Booty."

"Oh, is that my new nickname?" I asked, giggling.

"Yes, because I miss that booty."

"I miss you too. Once I get settled at work, let's set a date."

"Sounds good to me. Now I have something to look forward to."

"Me too. Love you, Everett. Chat later."

"Love you too. Bye for now."

Feeling uplifted after speaking with Everett, I called my mom.

"Hi, sweetie," she said. "Everything okay? Are you in Chicago?"

"Yes, I just got here. Mom, my apartment's amazing. I'm so happy with it!"

"That's good to hear. But we were pretty disappointed you couldn't make it home for a visit."

"I know, Mom. Things just got too hectic, and I didn't want to rush the visit. I promise I'll come home as soon as I can."

"Okay. Well, you must be exhausted after that long drive. I'll let you go. Let's talk tomorrow. I'm glad everything went well with the move."

"You know me, Mom. Organized Michelle," I said with a laugh. "I love you. Chat later."

"Bye, sweetie."

After I hung up, I texted Jennifer to let her know I arrived, completed the apartment inspection, and returned the move-in checklist to the property manager.

Chapter Thirteen

After a week in Chicago, I'd familiarized myself with my new neighborhood. Within walking distance from my apartment, I discovered a family-owned coffee shop, eateries, bars, and various clothing shops. I knew I'd love living and working in Chicago. Once I settled into my job, I planned to find affordable housing within an easy commute. As I sat in the kitchen reviewing job-related documents, my phone buzzed.

It was a text from Everett. Hi, Michelle, just landed. I'll call you when I get home. Love you.

His text invigorated me. I quickly typed a reply. Okay, luv. I miss you and can't wait to hear your voice.

Since it was a gorgeous Sunday afternoon with clear skies and a refreshing breeze, I decided to relax on the balcony to wait for Everett's call. As I absorbed the fabulous view, I admired the uniqueness of the architecture and the vista of skyscrapers displaying interesting colors. Flanking the traffic on the street below, clusters of people swarmed these remarkable buildings. I smiled because I'd soon join the flow of entering and exiting the JCI's building. I glanced at the time on my phone. Everett should be home by now.

I called him, but he didn't answer, so I left a message. Hey luv, just waiting for your call. Get back to me when you can.

It was out of character for Everett not to have called since he was always punctual, so I hoped nothing happened. After another hour, I started getting concerned. I called again, and this time, it went straight to voicemail. Hey, Everett, is everything okay? You should be home by now. Please call me!

As I waited for him to call, I got some salad and fruit from the kitchen and sat down to eat. When my phone buzzed, I was relieved to see his text.

Hey, babe, I'm home. I got stuck in traffic, and I went to the store to pick up a few things. Let me unpack, and I'll call you then.

My relief quickly turned to irritation. Once again, he couldn't take a moment to call rather than text. The more I dwelled on it, the more annoyed I became. This was starting to become a habit. I called Everett as soon as I got to Chicago. Was it too much to expect the same courtesy from him? Girl, get it together because if you don't, you're going to cuss his ass out!

I felt like hurtling the phone across the room. My appetite was gone. I put my food back in the fridge and tried to distract myself by watching TV. This wasn't how I wanted to start my life in Chicago, but I tried not to focus on it. Was I overreacting, or were my instincts trying to warn me? I wasn't sure, and I was angry that this even had to be an issue. I continue to channel surf. It seemed like an eternity before Everett finally called.

"Hey, babe, sorry for not calling sooner. I've eaten out for two weeks, so all I could think about was a good home-cooked meal."

By now, I was so furious that I didn't know how to respond. He couldn't call while driving or at the store, either? Really? I didn't want to be angry, but I was. Still, I'd let it go … for now.

"Well, I'm glad you made it home. I was starting to get worried. It's not like you not to call. We always stay in touch."

"I know, Michelle. I'm sorry. I'm tired, and I messed up. Can you please forgive me?"

"Everett, you're too much. You know I'm upset."

"I know. But big Everett can put a smile on that pretty face."

"I agree with that." I took a deep breath to ease the tension in my body. "What's for dinner?" I asked.

"Spaghetti and broccoli. Quick and easy. I want to eat, shower, and go to bed."

"If you'd flown back Friday, you'd have had the weekend to recuperate from the trip."

"That was my plan, but one of the instructors had an extra ticket to see Chris Botti, the trumpeter. I always wanted to see him in concert, so I bought the ticket from him and changed my return flight."

"Really? How was the concert?" I heard Everett running water into a pot.

"It was amazing. Now don't get jealous. I'll take you to see him."

"I'm not jealous. I'm glad you had a great time."

Something about his tone felt off, and it was happening a little too often for me. I couldn't explain it, but Everett knew Chris Botti was one of my favorite jazz musicians. Why didn't he tell me earlier about the concert? It was only a concert. What was the big deal?

"Everett, tomorrow's my first day at work, and I have to report at 9:30 a.m. I need to sort out my clothes and prepare for bed. I'm glad you're back. We'll talk later. Have a good evening."

"Okay, you too, babe. Chat later."

After I spoke with Everett, I decided not to dwell on the conversation. I didn't want to waste energy thinking about whether or not he was being honest, so I focused on preparing for my first day of work. I always strove for comfort with a minimalistic look that was confident and approachable. I laid out a red blazer, a pair of red, black, and gray plaid pants, a white V-neck tee shirt, and black loafers. As they said, first impressions were the lasting impressions. Feeling a little nervous and excited about work, I got ready for bed and tried not to think about Everett.

Before my 8:00 a.m. alarm the next morning, I woke to a cacophony of car horns. It was quite a startling reminder that I was no longer in the suburbs. Before I got out of bed, I said a quick prayer for God's presence to guide me through the day. When I saw that I still had plenty of time before I had to leave for work, I went to make my morning protein shake and sat on the balcony. Today, the weather was muggy with hazy skies. As I listened to the endlessly blowing horns, I realized I was starting a new chapter in my life, which deeply resonated with me. I felt confident that the day would go well. After finishing my shake, I went back inside and got ready for work.

Since I didn't want to be late navigating the traffic, I took an Uber and arrived at JCI at 9:15 a.m. The building was an elegant 40-story skyscraper. I walked into the building, checked in at the guard station to get a temporary badge, and proceeded to the elevator.

When the elevator arrived, I entered with a group of people. When several exited on the 4th floor, I exited also and reported to the Human Resources Department. A fit young man in his twenties greeted me with an infectious smile.

"Good morning! How can I help you?"

"I'm here to see Mrs. Runnels."

"Can you provide me with your name?"

"Ms. Michelle Davis."

"Thanks, Ms. Davis." He scanned his computer screen. "I'll let her know you're here. Please take a seat."

"Thank you."

I sat near the entrance door, which gave me a better view of the office. My observation of the environment was that the people were friendly and professional. Feeling a little anxious, I took out my phone for a distraction. A few moments later, a woman approached.

"Hi, Ms. Davis. I'm Mrs. Runnels. Welcome to JCI!"

An attractive brunette in her mid-thirties, she wore a blue pants suit accented by a white shirt, heels, and simple jewelry. Her long hair was swept back in a ponytail.

I rose, and we shook hands. "Thank you! I'm excited to be here."

"We're excited to have you here. Let's step into my office. How are you adjusting to Chicago?"

"Quite well. This isn't my first time here. I vacationed here a few years ago and thoroughly loved it."

"Agreed. There's an abundance of things to do in Chicago. I'm certain you'll love living here."

When we arrived at her desk, she flooded me with

questions and paperwork. Then she guided me to a computer to complete the lengthy onboarding process. After completing it, I returned to her desk. Mrs. Runnels told me to report to security to obtain my employee identification badge.

"Ms. Davis, after you get your badge, please return here, and I'll show you to your office. It should take about thirty minutes to get your badge. Do you have any questions for me?"

"Not at the moment."

"Okay, see you shortly."

∼

When I arrived at security, an older man who could have been Mr. Shelton's twin greeted me. From his warm smile, he seemed just as pleasant and he immediately made me feel at home.

"Hi, I'm Mr. Terry. You must be Ms. Davis."

"I am. Mrs. Runnels sent me here for my identification badge."

"You're in the right place. Take a seat in front of the white curtain. This should only take a few minutes."

I watched Mr. Terry working on his computer. "Almost done, Ms. Davis. Just a few more steps."

"No problem. I'm not in a hurry."

After a few moments, my stomach growled. Even though I had my morning shake, I was hungry. I reached into my purse and retrieved a breakfast bar.

Mr. Terry laughed. "That's almost like a rite of passage with new hires. Most are too nervous to eat before they come, and once they're here, they're shuffled from one office to another. Go ahead and enjoy your breakfast bar. I'll wait."

Slightly embarrassed, I made a mental note to ensure I

had a proper breakfast before coming to work in the future. I quickly freshened my lipstick and waited for Mr. Terry to take my picture.

"Okay, Ms. Davis, I entered all your information into the computer. Ready for your picture?"

"Yes."

"Okay, sit up straight."

Before I got the perfect smile on my face, he snapped the picture.

"Wasn't that a bit quick, Mr. Terry?" I asked.

"No worries. I've been doing this job for some time. Trust me. I know how to get a good picture."

After a few more clicks on his computer, out came my identification badge. I was pleasantly surprised to see how flattering the picture was, even in black and white.

"See, Ms. Davis? I told you not to worry. Your ID badge will allow you access in and out of the building and into the company's network and your computer. If you have any issues with your badge, please let me know. Have a pleasant day, and get some lunch soon! The first day's always the longest."

"Thanks, Mr. Terry. Have a good day."

I looked at my ID. I was official now and felt a sense of accomplishment. When I returned to Mrs. Runnels's office, she showed me to my office and handed me the keys.

When she opened the door, sunlight illuminated a spacious corner office with a fabulous city view. If I thought my apartment was amazing, my office was the stuff of dreams. Contemporarily furnished, it offered an executive desk with double computer screens, a keyboard, and a docking station with a laptop. The black ergonomic office chair looked comfortable enough to sleep on, and a rectangular table, six chairs, and wall-mounted television provided a convenient meeting venue. There was even a coat closet with shelves and a personal safe. Thriving plants, modern art, and accessories added an elegant finishing touch.

"Ms. Davis, the office supply room is three doors down. Please take whatever you need to set up your office."

"This is a lovely office," I said.

Mrs. Runnels smiled. "We pride ourselves in providing a great working environment." She glanced at her watch. "And since it's almost lunchtime, why don't you stop by my office at 1:30 so we can complete your in-processing? You'll find some great menu options in the staff canteen."

"Oh, I brought my lunch," I said. "Is there a lunchroom on this floor?"

"Next to the supply room. I'll see you later."

After Mrs. Runnels left, I took a few moments to absorb the environment before sitting at my desk. I noticed the computer was on and waiting for me to input my account information. Once logged in, I checked my inbox and noticed a schedule alert for a 3:00 p.m. team meeting with Janelle Brookdale. My first team meeting. I wasn't worried, as I was confident with my skills and didn't need validation from others. No matter what this opportunity brought, I was ready for any challenge.

Feeling hungry, I took my lunch bag and went to the lunchroom. Once again, the decor was stunning, and the view was equally impressive. As I warmed my meal in the microwave, two men and a woman in their late twenties or early thirties entered and sat at the nearest table to the entrance. Engaged in conversation, they didn't acknowledge me. As the new person, I felt somewhat awkward, so I introduced myself.

"Hi, I'm Michelle Davis. I started today."

In unison, they said, "Pleasure to meet you, Michelle."

The woman, a redhead with a dusting of freckles, said, "Hi, I'm Katie Allen. What section are you assigned to?"

"Major Acquisitions."

"Oh, you must be the new manager. The Director informed us about last week."

"Yes, I am."

"Well, I'd like to be the first, well, maybe not the first, to welcome you to JCI. I'm the Senior Contracts Specialist on your team. If you haven't been informed, today at 3:00 p.m., we're having a team meeting. See you there?"

"Yes, I saw the meeting on my schedule."

"Ms. Davis, let me introduce Richard Arts and Patrick James. Richard joined our team two weeks ago and is also a Senior Contracts Specialist on your team, and Patrick, known as the computer wizard, works in the IT department on the 7th floor."

Both rose to shake my hand.

"Look forward to working with you," Richard said.

"Same here," Patrick added.

I smiled, perhaps a little more than I should have. Both were almost ridiculously handsome, and they'd certainly be quite a work distraction. Girl, enough with the eye candy. You need to stop! Did you forget you're in a relationship? But what was wrong with looking? Men certainly had no problem with it.

As Richard sat down, I noticed how well-dressed he was. With his dark, Middle Eastern looks, he was quite debonair with dark eyes and dimples. He wore a checkered gray suit with straight-legged pants, a white t-shirt, and gray loafers. He was quite the bold fashion statement. I wondered if he was as proficient at his job as he was with his wardrobe.

Patrick's aura exuded warmth, confidence, and a touch of rebellion. He tempered his dramatic auburn 'frohawk with a beige shirt with rolled-up sleeves, stonewashed jeans, and Vans slip-ons.

"Richard, I'm looking forward to working with you. And, Patrick, now I know who to call if I have any computer issues," I said with a smile.

"Ms. Davis," Katie said. "If you need anything, you can find me on the global."

"Thanks," I said.

Feeling upbeat and more at home, I returned to my office and enjoyed my lunch.

Chapter Fourteen

After lunch, I went to the supply room. I'd never considered supply rooms exciting before, but I was in awe when I opened the door. I felt like I'd walked into an Office Depot. The neatly organized shelves were packed with desk organizers, triple-compartment desk trays, assorted paper in different colors, pens, pencils, and many other imaginable supplies. Everything I could ever need was in this room. I'd always been obsessed with a neat workspace and loathed it when people touched my things.

I recalled at my last job before I had my own office space. Whenever there was an office function, the party organizer played a game called, Whose Desk? Can You Guess? The objective was to guess whose desk the displayed item(s) belonged on. It was hilarious when the organizer asked, "Whose desk has one main item?" Everyone in the room shouted, "That's Michelle's desk!" The room erupted in laughter because I had a desk organizer with a Zebra pen, a pencil, and one yellow marker.

Everything else in my workspace had been neatly stowed in my desk drawers and cabinets, and everyone in the office knew not to sit in my chair or touch anything on my desk. Unfortunately, a co-worker found out the hard way when I came to work one day and noticed the Zebra pen on my desk was missing. I stood up and shouted, "Whoever took my fire trucking pen better return it right now!" I wanted to say my fucking pen, but I was in the office.

Shortly after, one of my co-workers appeared at my desk and said, "Michelle, I'm so sorry. I forgot to sign a document that I was presenting to the boss. When I walked past your desk, I borrowed your pen and forgot to put it back."

The office was silent as everyone waited to hear how I responded. I simply looked at her, took my pen, and sat back down. I hadn't even felt bad about how I reacted to the situation.

When I returned to my new office at JCI, with my clear desk organizer with matching desk trays, a notepad, one Zebra pen, and one mechanical pencil, I closed the door and smiled. Then I arranged the items I'd selected from the supply room neatly on my desk. I chuckled. Now that I had my office, I didn't have to concern myself with others invading my space, forcing me to cuss them out.

As I sat at my desk, I noticed the time on my computer was 1:15. So that I wouldn't be late for my 1:30 appointment with Mrs. Runnels, I gathered my belongings, locked the door, and walked to her office. After I completed the employment paperwork, she escorted me to the office of Ms. Janelle Brookdale, the Director of Contracts, my boss.

I was blown away by the view when I walked into her office. I thought I had a beautiful office with a spectacular view, but mine looked like a broom closet in comparison. I breathed in the soothing fragrance of lavender. A bank of thriving plants drank in the sunlight beaming through the windows. The room's focal point was a stunning conference table made of gray-veined marble, supported by V-shape steel legs and silver leather chairs. It complemented a contemporary black L-shaped desk with a matching bookcase and chair. From the bold artwork to the minimal accessories, her office resonated with authority.

"Hi, Ms. Brookdale," Mrs. Runnels said. "I'd like to introduce Ms. Michelle Davis, the newest manager for all of the Intel Acquisitions."

We shook hands. "Nice to meet you, Ms. Davis."

"Likewise," I responded, noting her firm grip.

"Ms. Davis, if you need anything, you know where my office is. Again, welcome to JCI."

"Thank you, Mrs. Runnels." She left the room, closing the door behind her.

Ms. Brookdale motioned me to take a seat at the conference table. She retrieved some printouts from her neatly organized desk and sat down across from me. My first impression of her was that she was reserved, professional, and focused. She looked to be in her early fifties, and I noted that her immaculate, if eclectic, retro dress style didn't quite fit the image of the typical director position. Her caramel skin was beautiful, and her Halle Berry side-parted pixie hairstyle flattered her sculpted facial features and expressive brown eyes.

"Ms. Davis, do you mind if I call you Michelle?"

I shook my head. "Not at all."

"Good, then please address me as Janelle. In management, we're on a first-name basis. I'd like to welcome you to the team. As the manager overseeing all of JCI's 2.5 billion Intel acquisitions I expect you will have questions. So, I'll provide you with a list of your responsibilities and my expectations. Please feel free to ask me any questions after you have read it."

Janelle handed me the printouts. Inwardly, I jumped for joy when I noticed JCI used a Maxi-flex work schedule and remote work. Office hours were from 6:00 a.m. to 6:00 p.m. OMG! This was a blessing! I always loved the flexibility of setting my hours because I'm more productive and satisfied when I can control when and where I work. A flex-work schedule always created a great work-life balance for me and provided an immense sense of freedom.

"Michelle, I'm certain you'll have questions, but we have a 3:00 p.m. meeting where I'll introduce you to your team. After the meeting, please review the list, note your questions, and return to my office at 3:45 p.m."

It was apparent by all the work-related awards displayed in Janelle's office that she was established and respected by her peers. By her demeanor, I knew that when it came to my performance, excuses would be unacceptable. I wasn't concerned because I always stayed focused on my work goals in the office, which enabled me to excel in my career.

Janelle rose. "Shall we go?"

I followed her to the conference room further down the hall. When we entered yet another strikingly decorated room, the chatter I heard as we approached the door faded to silence. I immediately realized everyone knew Janelle meant business and wouldn't tolerate anything less than complete professionalism.

Eleven men and eight women sat attentively at a rectangular white conference table with yellow, steel-framed chairs. The room was decorated with a few plants and pieces of artwork. I placed my belongings on a table next to the door and stood quietly next to Janelle.

"Good afternoon, everyone," she said in a clear and commanding voice. "I wanted to introduce you to Ms. Michelle Davis, your team's manager."

A chorus of welcomes greeted me. I responded accordingly.

"Ms. Davis is highly experienced in the acquisition field," Janelle continued. "I'm confident she'll bring innovative ideas and new energy to our team." She turned to me. "Ms. Davis, on behalf of the JCI family, we look forward to working with you. Is there anything you'd like to say to your team?"

What the hell? Did she just put me on blast? I just met them. What did she expect me to say at this point? I sighed inwardly. Fortunately, public speaking was one of my strong points.

I smiled and took a moment to make eye contact with everyone. "First, I'd like to say how wonderful it is to meet you all. I worked at Marcell Technologies, Inc. for several years as a senior contract specialist before I accepted this position. I organized their annual acquisition training conferences, conducted training, was the central point of contact for all government-related contracts, set up recruiting events, and spearheaded the mentorship program. I'm excited to be a team member of JCI, as the interviewing team spoke highly about this team in my interview. I'm certain with our combined experiences; our team will achieve great results." I turned to Janelle and motioned that I had finished speaking.

"Thanks, Michelle. Team, I have to return to my office as I have another meeting to attend."

She was certainly a woman of few words, but her expression spoke volumes.

∼

After Janelle left the room, the chatter resumed. Standing in a room of people I had only just met and who didn't know I wasn't that sociable, I felt it important to take control. I never cared for mindless conversation. Just like Janelle, I was focused on the job and nothing else.

"Can I have everyone's attention, please?" I stated, noting how quickly the room silenced. "I'm looking forward to learning more about each of you and your duties and responsibilities. I'm certain you'll have questions for me, just as I'll have for you, but those will have to wait since I have a meeting at 3:45 pm with Ms. Brookdale. Thanks for the warm welcome, and enjoy the rest of your workday."

I quickly gathered my belongings. I had only twenty minutes to review Ms. Brookdale's list and write down my questions. When I returned to my office and checked my computer, I noticed an email from Janelle. "Hi, Michelle, please email your questions, and we'll meet tomorrow at 10:00 a.m. to discuss your questions and work schedule. For the remainder of the week, please report to work at 8:00 a.m."

Since my meeting with Janelle was canceled, I reviewed the list of responsibilities and her expectations. I realized immediately that my job as the manager would be challenging, but a challenge I welcomed. I compiled my questions and emailed them back to Janelle. Noting the time on the computer, I couldn't believe it was already time to go home. It was a blessing that I thoroughly enjoyed my work, and the salary was a bonus. Although I'd always been career-driven and not particularly sociable, I constantly strove to create a synergistic work environment. I felt it was also important for everyone, regardless of their pay grade, to understand that their voice mattered. This approach contributed to my successful career.

During the first two weeks on the job, I reviewed JCI's Standard Operation Procedures and met with Janelle to discuss my role in the company. She was clear, and to the point that she expected excellence, and if I needed her assistance, she expected me to research a solution before consulting her. She had an open-door policy, but not for pointless conversation. She declared that innovation was the key to being successful. Her statement wasn't new to me because that's how I had operated in all my previous jobs. As we talked, I felt like I saw a reflection of myself. Just as I was career-driven, meticulous, accomplished, detail-oriented, straightforward, ambitious, and organized, so was she. She emanated the same excellence and more.

I wondered if she prioritized her career over romance and whether she was divorced, in a relationship, or single. The only way I'd ever find out would be at the water cooler because she didn't mix her personal and work life. Since I never was a water cooler person, I'd probably never know, and truthfully, it wasn't that important.

My goal was to build an enduring relationship with Everett. Although Janelle and I shared similar characteristics, I didn't want to be alone when I reached my fifties. Even though Everett and I talked and facetimed often, I hadn't seen him in person for over a month, and with my busy work schedule, it would likely be another two weeks before I did. While sitting at my desk one afternoon, I decided to call him.

"Hey, booty, how's it going?"

"Busy, but no complaints. I love my job. But I'd like to start looking for a place. Can you come and help me look?"

"I can't think of anything more I'd like than to reacquaint myself with that juicy booty," he said with a laugh. "So, yes, I can come for a visit."

"Everett, this booty needs some attention, and you've definitely been starring in my dreams!" I stared out my office window. "But the only time we can look for a place is after work and on the weekend."

"No problem. I'll come for two weeks. That way, we'll have plenty of time to search for a place and get reacquainted."

"That sounds great! When can you come?"

"Let's look at next weekend. I'll schedule my leave and fly out on a Friday. Just be ready because Daddy's going to make up for the missed time with you. I'll book my flight when we hang up."

I felt a shiver at the thought of his touch and smell. "I really, really need you to hold me. It's been over a month."

Everett chuckled. "Oh, babe, I'm going to do much more than just hold you!"

"Keep this up," I whispered, "and I won't sleep tonight."

"Then catch up on your sleep now because we won't get much once I'm there."

I tried to banish the heat rising to my face. Easy girl, you're at work. Keep those hormones in check!

"Point taken. Guess we'd better stop before neither of us gets anything done. And Everett, I'm very excited to see you again. I've missed you so much."

"So am I. I'll text you later."

About an hour after we hung up, Everett texted me his itinerary. "Hey, babe, I'll be there next Friday at 6:00 p.m. Can't wait to see you."

Chapter Fifteen

Everett had purchased his airline ticket, and in anticipation of his visit, I felt a sexy outfit was warranted. Two days before he arrived, I visited Victoria's Secret and bought a black crotchless lace teddy that tantalizingly exposed my cheeks. Everett always went wild when I walked around wearing only heels and a thong. When he arrived, I planned to go straight home after work, freshen up, and present his very own welcome basket to sample.

As I worked at my desk, I received a message on the office chat messenger from Janelle that read, "Michelle, when you're free, please come to my office."

I replied, "I'll be there in five minutes." I saved the memo I was working on and went to her office.

I knocked on the door. "Hi, Janelle, you wanted to see me?"

Janelle briefly glanced up and motioned me to come in and take a seat, only then did I realize she was on a call. I felt embarrassed and foolish for not noticing. I settled into a black leather chair in front of her desk. The relaxed but measured tone of her voice relayed quiet assertion. Although I tried not to listen to the conversation, I noticed her precise enunciation of each word. It was clear I had to be on point when talking with her.

After Janelle finished her call, she said, "I won't keep you long, Michelle. I just wanted to let you know that upper management is quite impressed with your performance and would like to offer you the opportunity to take the lead and manage the mentoring program."

While I was flattered, I had no desire to get involved.

"Janelle, I'm delighted my performance has been noticed, but I spearheaded the mentoring program at my last job, which was rather time-consuming. Maybe in a few months when I'm more settled in the job, I'll consider it, but for now, I respectfully decline."

Janelle thoughtfully watched me. I noticed how her nails were always beautifully manicured. She was meticulous in both appearance and attitude.

"No problem at all, Michelle. I respect your openness and decision. Honestly, most would have agreed and accepted the position because they wouldn't want to disappoint management. I feel you're going to do quite well here. Let's discuss it again in a few months."

"Sounds good to me. I'll note it on my calendar. Is there anything else?"

"No. Enjoy the rest of your day."

"You too, Janelle."

Before I returned to my office, I stopped in the ladies' room. Katie was drying her hands and was turning to leave when she saw me.

"Hi, Ms. Davis."

"Hi, Katie."

For a moment, it looked like she wanted to say something else, but she simply walked past me. I got a distinct impression that I intimidated her, but to be honest, I preferred brevity to pointless talk. When I saw her at lunch or on a break, she was always the chattiest person around. I had no complaints about Katie. She was a good team member, but I found her a little too loud for my taste.

On my way back to my office, I bumped into Richard.

"Hi, Richard. How's it going?"

"Busy as always, Ms. Davis. And you?"

"Busy but good. That's the way I like it. Well, enjoy the rest of your day, and if you ever need my assistance, please let me know."

"Thanks, Ms. Davis. I will."

I glanced over my shoulder as he walked away. He always looked like he was ready to walk the runway. Today, he wore a single-breasted checkered gray and white jacket, blue polo shirt, and slim-fit olive jeans. OMG, he's gorgeous! Girl, you need to stop. You're his boss, not some teenager swooning over her crush. But, damn, this man could stop traffic with his looks. I distracted myself with my phone and noticed it was almost lunch. When I returned to my office, I placed the "I'm At Lunch" sign on my door, retrieved my southwest salad and chicken sandwich from my lunch bag, and watched The Tamron Hall Show on my phone.

As I ate my lunch, my phone buzzed. It was a text from Everett. Hey, babe, I'm here. Instead of texting back, I called him.

"Hi, luv! I thought you were arriving after I got off work?"

"I wanted to surprise you. Why don't you call the property manager to let me in, or I can come by your office and pick up the key."

I glanced at the clock on my computer. I was happy to hear from Everett, but his timing couldn't have been worse. Damn! So much for my plan to surprise him!

"I'd love to see you," I replied, "but I have to attend the team progress check meeting in an hour. I'll call the apartment concierge."

"Works for me. Text me the address, and I'll Uber to your place."

"Okay, I'll text it now."

My fingers fumbled from excitement as I typed the address. "I wish I could leave now! I've missed you so much."

"What time do you get off work?"

"Four-thirty."

"Okay, see you soon. Bye, booty."

After speaking with Everett, I found it impossible to concentrate. I longed for his touch but knew I had to control my emotions, particularly the hunger in my body. But try as I might, all I could think about was his smell and lying in his arms. As I sat fantasizing, I glanced at the computer clock and noticed that the meeting would start in ten minutes. Damn, I was too distracted and had to get it together before heading to the meeting. I secured my computer, locked my door, and proceeded to the conference room. Halfway there, I met Janelle in the hallway.

"Good afternoon, Janelle."

"Hello, Michelle. Are you getting settled on the job?"

"Yes, I am. Thanks for asking."

"Well, if you need my assistance, just let me know."

"Will do."

I was glad we reached the conference room because the exchange felt somewhat awkward. As we entered, everyone was seated at the table. The energy in the room felt unenthusiastic, as most were ready to end the workday and start their weekend. I noticed an empty chair next to where Janelle would sit, so I sat there while she went to the front of the table and began speaking.

"Team, I won't keep you long. I want to inform you that I'll be out of the office next Wednesday on a short-notice business trip for two weeks. So please email your progress status summaries to me no later than 2:30 on Monday, and courtesy copy Ms. Davis, as she'll be in charge while I'm away."

Janelle must have noticed the puzzled look on my face because she said, looking at me, "I know this is short notice, Michelle, but don't worry, I'll brief you Monday morning."

I forced myself to remain calm, but inside, I was screaming. This cannot be happening! I don't want to think about work this weekend. I want to focus on Everett. Trying to remain professional, I nodded my head.

Janelle glanced at everyone at the table. "Does anyone have any other questions?"

No one said a word.

"Very well. This concludes our meeting. Enjoy your weekend."

As everyone filed out of the room, Janelle motioned me to stay.

"I apologize for the short notice," she explained, "but if I didn't have the confidence that you could run the office, I would have managed via email. Like I said, don't worry. I'm very detailed, and I'll provide a step-by-step outline of my duties that need to be handled while I'm away."

"Janelle, I'm not worried. Just caught off guard."

"I know you were. I was only notified three hours ago. But there's nothing to worry about. I'll be just an email or phone call away."

"Well, that's reassuring. I look forward to sitting down with you on Monday."

"Very well. Let's wrap this up. Have a great weekend."

"You too, Janelle," I said and left the room.

When I returned to my office, I sat down and put my head in my hands. I took a few deep breaths until I felt calmer. It wasn't filling in for Janelle, which left me feeling frustrated. It was the time limitations the extra responsibilities would place on my time with Everett. But I had to accept that there was nothing I could change. It was part of my job and part of being in charge. The only thing I could change was my thinking.

I said a mental prayer. Michelle, you got this. You've always succeeded in overcoming challenges, so you're not about to fail now. With a more positive attitude and finally free from distractions, I organized next week's workload and ended my day feeling upbeat. Eager to get home to Everett, I changed into my sneakers, locked my office, and left.

I approached the elevator and saw a crowd of people waiting, so I took the stairs. By the time I reached the first floor, I was damn near out of breath. Girl, you need to get your ass back in the gym! I chuckled to myself as I approached my car and pressed the button on the handle to open it. Nothing happened. I pressed the button again, but the door wouldn't open. Irritated, I reached into my bag for the remote. Nothing. Where the hell was it? Frantically, I searched my bag, then I remembered. Damn! I left the remote in my desk drawer. Earlier, I'd gone to my car to get a folder I needed for the staff meeting and put the remote in my desk drawer instead of my jacket pocket.

Nice work, girl! Back I went into the building, but this time, I took the elevator. As usual, it took forever to come. While I paced, Katie walked past me.

"Ms. Davis aren't you going in the wrong direction?" she said with a smile. "The workday is over."

I didn't want to mention that I'd forgotten the remote. "I know. I just came back for my laptop. Work first, play later."

"Okay, Ms. Davis. Don't work too hard this weekend."

When the elevator finally arrived, I was relieved that it went straight to the 4th floor. By now, the building must have been pretty empty. When I got to my office, I made sure I didn't rush. I got the remote and my laptop. When I returned to the garage, I practically sprinted to my car. Lord, please, no more delays. I had to get home to Everett!

It didn't take long to get out of the garage, but getting through Chicago rush hour traffic was another story. Still, that was part of working in the city, so there was no point in stressing over it. It was Friday evening, and the streets bustled with people and street performances, and businesses brightened their storefronts to entice shoppers. People hurried to their favorite bar or restaurant in the hope of beating the commuter rush or simply arriving in time for happy hour to celebrate the end of the week.

As I navigated the traffic, I rolled down my back windows to absorb the pulse of the city but then quickly rolled them back up because the car fumes were overwhelming. I noticed a group of people watching a young man on the corner drumming on a set of pots and pans. From what I heard; he sounded pretty good. All the surrounding excitement was exhilarating, and I wanted Everett and me to experience it together as we explored the city.

I tried to control my frustration, but it finally got the best of me. I was constantly bogged down by slow or inattentive drivers. There seemed to be an endless number of cars and trucks with the drivers blowing their horns. I had to wonder how they thought blowing their horns would make the traffic flow faster. If that were the case, I'd blow the hell out of my horn. Normally, I just relaxed and flowed with the traffic, but today was different. Everett was in town! To calm my nerves, I selected Chris Stapleton on my Apple playlist and grooved to the music. While I sat in traffic, I called Everett.

"Hey, Everett, I'm on my way home. Traffic's crazy, but I should be there shortly."

"No problem. I'm just watching TV. I have to say you have the most fantastic view!"

"Yes, isn't it something? And it's amazing at night. Did you eat?"

"I scrounged around the fridge and made a sandwich."

"Okay, I'll be there soon. If you're still hungry …"

Everett chuckled. "Oh, you know I'm hungry, babe, but not for another sandwich."

I felt a rush of heat throughout my body. At this rate, I'd have to crank up the air conditioning.

"Stop!" I said. "The hotter I get, the slower this damn traffic moves!"

"Don't worry, babe. We'll make up for the lost time when you get here …"

A block from my apartment, I pressed the voice command and texted Everett. Hey, luv, be there in two minutes.

By the time I pulled into my parking space, I felt like an animal in heat. I hadn't had sex in over three weeks. I almost had to laugh at myself. Seriously, Michelle? Calm yourself down! It's not like you moved to a convent! I managed to maintain a sense of decorum as I hurried to the elevator. For once, it came straight away, so I took a few moments to take some deep breaths before getting out on my floor. My heart pounded with excitement as I unlocked the door and saw Everett naked on the sectional. I froze and stared. Talk about a homecoming surprise!

"What are you waiting for?" he whispered with a smile.

"Everett …!"

"Michelle, just shut the door."

I shut it and dropped my stuff on the table. When I went to him, he pulled me onto his lap and passionately kissed me. I felt his hardness press against me.

"Everett … I need to freshen up."

More firmly, Everett kissed me, and I felt my resolve draining away. I pulled back, looked into his seducing eyes, and noticed he had his braces removed. Yes, he was handsome, but I knew getting his teeth fixed would take him to a new level. He looked damn good!

"Everett, when did you get your braces off? Why didn't you tell me?"

"I wanted it to be a surprise. Now, stop asking me questions. You're killing me, babe. Just get your shower, and don't take too long."

"Okay, okay. I won't."

I rushed to the bedroom and took a shower in record time. Barely drying myself off, I slipped into my black laced teddy and heels and returned to Everett. He smiled, his eyes lingering hungrily on my body.

"Damn, Michelle, you look amazing! Turn around and let me get a good look at that tight ass."

I slowly turned around while glancing over my shoulder

at him, and then I bent down and wiggled my hips to give him a better look. His groan said it all. Everett motioned me to sit on the sectional. He knelt on the floor in front of me, and with his beautiful smile and no braces, he spread my, legs, and kissed my throbbing sweet spot. I moaned and sank helplessly against the pillows.

"I've missed you so much."

"Shh," Everett whispered, pressing his fingers against my lips. "Don't speak."

I writhed and moaned with every magical touch of Everett's mouth and fingers.

"Don't stop! Please … I'm going to …"

I bit my lip and filled him with my nectar. We took our time, savoring every moment, every touch, until we finally fell asleep exhausted in each other's arms.

Chapter Sixteen

Over the next couple of weeks, the June temperatures soared to the high 90s. To avoid the muggy heat, Everett and I stayed in as much as possible and searched Zillow for my dream home with a maximum forty-minute commute. I wanted a two-story house with 3-4 bedrooms, 3.5 baths, a two-car garage, and a private backyard, as Everett and I enjoyed making love outside. I found several houses on Zillow but didn't want to commute for an hour because an hour in Chicago could quickly turn into an hour and a half or more.

I loved the excitement of city life, but living in my apartment was challenging when it came to hauling groceries from my car to the apartment. And while I adored the view and city lights, the constant noise was becoming tiresome. After several searches, I chose three homes and contacted the realtor to get the lockbox access codes to view them on Saturday.

On Saturday morning, Everett spooned and awakened me with a very hard surprise.

"Good morning, beautiful," he murmured, nuzzling my neck.

I yawned and smiled. "Is this my wake-up call?"

"Isn't it better than an alarm?" he chuckled.

He gently squeezed my breasts, pulled down my night shorts, and filled me with his glorious sunshine. Afterward, we snuggled together, simply enjoying each other's company.

"I love how you wake me up in the morning, Everett. That's exactly what I needed to start my day."

Everett chuckled. "Babe, you know I aim to please. I'm going to make some coffee. You want some?"

"No, but you can turn on the kettle. I'm going to shower and have some green tea after. It will be hot today, so I'm glad we arranged to view the homes early."

"It's going to be a scorcher. Welcome to Chicago!"

In the shower, my skin still tingled from Everett's touch. I stood beneath the cool jets of water and enjoyed the refreshing feel of the streaming water. Everett slipped into the shower behind me, turned me toward him, and silently knelt between my legs. I moaned and caressed his shoulders. Enveloped in the cool water, Everett lifted me against the wall and slowly slid inside me. Lost in our passion, we rocked together until we climaxed in unison. We sank onto the tiles and let the water cool us.

"Babe," I said, kissing Everett, "if we continue, we're not looking at any houses today."

He laughed and trailed his lips down my neck. "Babe, I know. But you taste like strawberries, and I can't get enough of you."

"Okay, but we can't stay in the shower all morning. Did you forget that we're looking at the first house at 10:00 a.m.?"

"No, I haven't forgotten. Then you'd better get ready. Seeing you naked excites me, and you know how that goes…"

~

After we got ready, Everett fixed his coffee and my tea and put them in spill-proof mugs. The Chicago heat felt like a swamp when we reached the parking garage. Sweat instantly prickled my skin.

"Damn, Everett, it's already hot." I wiped some perspiration off my forehead.

"That's an understatement. I'm glad we decided to wear shorts."

When we got to my car, Everett opened the door and waited for me to get situated. As soon as he got in and started the car, he cranked up the AC.

"That feels so much better!" I said.

Everett drove out of the garage. "What's the schedule for today?"

"Ten, noon, and four. I figured an hour would be enough to view each home and then grab lunch. I wanted to space them closer, but knowing the traffic, I didn't want to miss any appointments."

As Everett merged into the traffic, I input the first address into the GPS, then selected the Neo-soul station on the radio. Everett shook his head as we inched along.

"Look at this traffic, and it's still early! Babe, you sure you want to deal with this every day?"

"That's why I want to find a place near the Metro station," I replied, looking out the window. "No way do I want to drive to work in this every day."

"Let's hope you find a place that meets all your requirements," he said.

~

As Everett drove to the first house, we sipped our drinks, or at least we tried to. He swore under his breath as he constantly slowed, sped up, and hit the brakes.

"Dammit!" he yelled. "These fools sure as hell don't know how to drive."

I squeezed his arm. "Everett, the traffic isn't that bad. Just slow down and relax. We left early, so there's no rush."

"Babe, I know. But it's crazy. No one knows what they're doing."

"Okay, then why don't I drive back when we're done?"

"I'm absolutely cool with that," he said.

Although the morning was stifling, once we escaped the traffic, the drive out of the city was beautiful. Businesses flipped their closed sign to open, morning joggers and walkers were out, and the panorama of dramatic skyscrapers dominated the distant skyline. The more I absorbed the view, the more excited I became to be part of a city filled with so much to offer, all of which I hoped Everett and I would soon experience together.

We arrived at the first house a few minutes before 10:00 a.m. The neighborhood was quiet and full of beautiful homes. As we pulled into the driveway, I was impressed by the authentic Tudor-style home with red brick and white and black trim. I particularly liked the lush front yard and full-width front porch. I already imagined sitting there with my morning coffee, listening to the birds. When we walked inside, a cozy foyer opened up the home's uniqueness, and the brown, solid oak flooring gleamed from sunlight streaming through the windows.

The open-concept living room was perfect for entertaining. A stepped, double-sided soft gray brick fireplace separated the white kitchen from the living room. One side of the fireplace was designed to accommodate a flat-screen television and even had storage for firewood. I envisioned Everett and I curled up in front of it on a cold winter's day. The kitchen was equally striking, with glass cabinets offset by a gray granite countertop.

We proceeded through the kitchen, and I opened the patio doors that led to the vast, private, and perfectly manicured backyard. Just the thought of watching Everett prepare dinner on the deck kitchen called my name.

"So, what do you think of this yard?" Everett asked.

"It's well-kept but a lot of work. I'd definitely have to hire a landscaping company."

Everett pointed to the fence. "You'll have all the privacy you want with that high fence."

"Maybe, but from the look of the fence, it needs to be replaced."

"Which will be expensive," Everett said.

"Let's see what the rest of the house looks like," I responded and walked back into the kitchen.

Although the home was lovely, the ivory-painted bedrooms were smaller than I had envisioned. The main level had a standard bedroom and full bathroom, which was great for guests, and there were three additional bedrooms on the upper level. The master bedroom looked more spacious in the pictures, and the dark gray and white bathroom felt claustrophobic. The bonus was a large walk-in closet. Down the hall from the main bedroom were two smaller bedrooms with narrow walk-in closets that could be utilized as an office or a bedroom. The two bedrooms shared the Jack and Jill bathroom, which was beautifully designed with blue vanities, a white sink countertop, a framed white and blue square mirror mounted over each sink, and a frosted glass shower for privacy. Across from the bathroom, there was a laundry room neatly tucked away behind double doors.

After inspecting the rest of the house, we spent a couple of minutes on the front porch.

"So, what do you think?" Everett asked.

"It's a lovely house, but the bedrooms are rather small."

Everett nodded. "I agree. But you're less than thirty minutes from downtown, which is what you wanted."

"I know. Being close to work is a priority. And I love the backyard. Very private."

"This one has ticked off most of the boxes on your list," Everett said. "Let's lock up and head to the next house."

Before we left, I took a few pictures of the house to compare later. Unfortunately, the drive to the next house became a crawl, and Everett's frustration increased.

"Hey, babe, why don't you pull over and let me drive?" I suggested.

"No point now," he said. "We're only about half an hour away. I should have grabbed a breakfast bar."

I didn't want his stress to spoil the mood, so I turned the station to cool jazz.

"Thanks, babe. I need some calming music."

Due to the traffic, half an hour turned into an hour. We arrived at the next house at 12:15 p.m. This meant if we wanted to grab lunch and make our next appointment, we had to rush. On the drive, I noticed the location's convenience to local restaurants and grocery stores, and the Metrorail, CTA stations, and highways were fairly close.

As we drove down a gorgeous, tree-lined street, I spotted the two-story, L-shaped, prairie-style home. It was a lovely Amherst gray with off-white brick, a charcoal roof, and a two-car garage. The sturdy brick column lent a unique quality and was complemented by beautiful green shrubs near the entrance. The home felt rich and was certainly eye-catching.

"This is gorgeous!" I exclaimed. "What do you think?"

"I agree. And did you see the remote-controlled gate leading to the garage and backyard?"

"Yes, I did. It seems like a quiet neighborhood, which is definitely a plus, and the trees are so grand, leafy, and green, and you know we enjoy our after-dinner walks. Let's go inside and take a look around the place."

After inputting the access code, we entered a warm, spacious, 4-bedroom, 3.5-bath home. The natural white oak hardwood flooring was immaculate, and it was evident that the previous owner took great pride in maintaining it. The soft white paint accented an open living room with an adjoining kitchen. A gray rectangular free-standing island with a morning rose granite countertop dominated the center of the kitchen, along with stainless steel appliances.

The windows flooded the space, allowing natural light to radiate throughout the room. What caught my attention was the stunning gold light fixture that graced the dining room. This area was brilliantly structured as a conversational space. The guest bedroom and bathroom were adjacent to the living room. The layout was perfect, as the bedroom had an access door that led to the bathroom. It was private and convenient for guests.

After I viewed the kitchen and living room, I took a few pictures on my phone as my mind flowed with decorating ideas.

With a huge smile, I said, "Everett, this kitchen is amazing! I know just how I'd decorate it."

"It's quite spectacular," he agreed.

"I can't wait to see the bedrooms," I said. "Let's head upstairs."

Two steps to the landing and eleven steps later, I knew

I'd found my dream home. On the upper level were three bedrooms and two baths. I proceeded down the hallway into an exquisite soft white main bedroom, full bathroom with gray and white Carrara Venato flooring and an enormous walk-in closet. I loved the simplicity of the dual sink, walk-in shower, jacuzzi tub, and separate room for the toilet. While I stood there daydreaming, Everett called out to me.

"Michelle, we've got to go. If we stay here longer, we might miss the next appointment."

"I know, but this home is beautiful. Let me look at the other rooms, and then we'll check out the basement."

"Okay, just make it quick."

I quickly looked at the other bedrooms and bathroom. They were standard bedrooms with walk-in closets that matched the color scheme of the main bedroom. The bathroom's soft white and blue tones were quite serene, which was a plus as I loved the color blue. The basement was the last stop before we left. While it was small and unfinished, it had a half bath and a laundry room.

While the house's interior was impressive, I was stunned by the lush shade trees flanking a beautiful outdoor oasis when we walked through the patio doors to the backyard. A two-tiered deck with a built-in canopy overlooked an enclosed yard lined with blooming flower beds, and the wood privacy fence was a bonus. The only negative for this house was the unfinished basement, which would be an extra expense. We made our way back to the entrance, and I snapped more pictures.

"Everett, I love this house! It ticks all the boxes."

"It does, but the basement is small and unfinished."

"I know, but it's adorable and feels like my home."

"Okay, I understand. Let's look at the last house, and then we can make a decision."

We're going to make the decision. I don't think so. If

I'm buying it, it's my decision.

"Also, the location is perfect," I said. "Less than a 30-minute drive to work."

"I get it, but we need to go," Everett said. "The traffic's only going to get worse, and I didn't plan on spending all day driving."

We quickly locked up and left. Before going to the third home, we had enough time to grab lunch. Everett had a hankering for fried chicken, so we googled the best place to eat and settled on Luella's Southern Kitchen.

Chapter Seventeen

Thirty minutes later, we arrived at Luella's Southern Kitchen restaurant. Since the restaurant was a storefront establishment, we had to find a place to park and walk in the scorching heat. Fortunately, Everett spotted a parking garage close to the restaurant. Although it was only a three-minute walk, it felt like an eternity in the smoldering heat. We were somewhat dismayed to see the line out the door when we got there, but from the intoxicating aroma wafting onto the street, I understood why there was a line. Everett went inside to speak with the hostess.

When he returned, he said, "Babe, the wait for a table will be at least an hour. It's 2ish now. If we wait, we'll miss the next appointment. Let's find a KFC or Popeye's Chicken. We can always come back another time."

Everett and I drove around and searched for the nearest KFC or Popeye's Chicken, and we ended up at Popeye's. It seemed like long lines were the order of the day because, when we got there, the line was also long. We parked and went inside. I went to the ladies' room and then found a table while Everett waited in line.

As I watched Everett, I felt a surge of excitement about getting home to spend time with him. This Chicago heat had me sweating in places I didn't know I could sweat, but with Everett, I felt a different, slower burning of heat. When he returned with our food, we discussed the two homes we viewed.

"So, Michelle, which house did you like best?"

"The second one. It had everything I wanted and more. We can do whatever we like in the backyard with that high fence." I glanced seductively at Everett.

"You're right about that, but do you want to buy a house with an unfinished basement?"

"That's not a deal-breaker. And I don't think it will be that expensive. I certainly don't need to worry about renovating it straight away."

"Well, it's your decision." Everett took a sip of his drink.

I thought, You're damn right. It's my decision.

"And we still have one more house to view."

Feeling slightly irritated, I said, "Let's see how that goes."

As we left the restaurant, I noticed traffic was at a standstill, "Babe, you want me to drive?"

Everett acquiesced. "Works for me."

I offered, as I wasn't in the mood to hear him complain about the traffic. I picked an upbeat station to keep me relaxed, programmed the GPS, and headed toward the freeway. My heart sank when I saw a sea of cars jamming the lanes.

I looked at the GPS and noticed that the ETA was 3:45

p.m. Thankfully, I'd anticipated traffic and rescheduled the last appointment for 4:00 p.m. Assuming there were no major delays, we should get there in time. I glanced at Everett and noticed he was asleep. I sighed with relief. At least he wouldn't start complaining again. I turned down the music and crept onto the freeway. The traffic was chaos. Frustrated drivers weaved in and out of lanes, and some even tried overtaking on the shoulder. After twenty minutes of crawling, the traffic finally accelerated, and I pulled into a curved driveway five minutes after 4:00 p.m.

I parked and tapped Everett on the shoulder.

"Hey, Luv, we're here."

"Huh, what?" he asked, groggily looking around.

"We're here. You slept the entire time."

"Babe, I'm sorry. It must have been the heat and lunch."

"No worries, I managed."

We sat in the car for a few minutes, assessing the house.

"The architecture of this home is fantastic," Everett said. "I love the elegant mix of red brick, dark gray roof, and light gray siding. Let's go in."

I had to agree. The 4-bedroom, 3-5 bath Georgian home was a masterpiece and absolutely stunning. After Everett entered the access code, we opened the door to a large foyer. Once inside, we were greeted by a spectacular sun-drenched formal living room with a sparkling crystal chandelier.

"Wow! Nice touch!" Everett exclaimed.

"It's beautiful," I said in awe. "And look how the sunlight sparkles off the crystals."

Adjacent to the living room was a guest bedroom. We opened the door into an ivory-painted room with a stretch ceiling and a small walk-in closet. The bonus was the door that led to an impeccably decorated black and white guest bathroom. Everett loved the design, and so did I. After we viewed the room, we headed to the chef-designed kitchen. Being the better cook, he fell in love with the kitchen straightway, and his eyes widened when he spotted the three-season room.

"Oh, Michelle, can't you just see us enjoying a drink and a smoke in this room?"

"Absolutely!"

"This is undeniably the house for you."

I pretended not to hear him and walked to the double French doors leading to a lovely backyard. I was disappointed to see that although the yard was beautiful, there was little to no privacy, and I had a clear view of the neighboring backyards. I made a mental note as we continued to a fully finished basement with a recreation room, a built-in bar, and another wood-burning fireplace.

After we viewed the basement, Everett said, "Yes! I can turn this room into my man cave."

Again! He's assuming that I'm buying a house to suit him. That's even if I buy this place.

Everett walked around like a child about to unwrap his Christmas presents. "This is perfect! What do you think about this as my man cave?"

"It can also be a gym or home theater," I suggested, struggling to keep the irritation from my voice.

"Oh, Michelle, stop. You know this will be my area."

"Let's look at the rest of the house," I said, cutting the conversation short.

We returned upstairs and walked up a winding staircase with a wrought iron banister that led to three spacious bedrooms on the second level. The large main suite was jaw-dropping gorgeous and featured ivory walls, large windows, a cozy sitting room, and two walk-in closets.

Designed for two, the main bathroom was stunningly decorated in tones of gray and white. It had a double bathroom vanity, a stone walk-in shower and tub, and a separate toilet room. Each additional bedroom and bathroom also offered an equally striking design. It was apparent that the previous owner put a lot of love and expense into the home.

Everett excitedly looked around. "Michelle, I know I keep repeating myself, but this one is my favorite. Close to the metro, shopping, and less than thirty-five minutes from your job."

Yes, you're repeating yourself, Everett …

His constant raving about the house was becoming annoying, and I didn't like being pressured, especially when I was making the decision.

"It's gorgeous," I said. "But there's no backyard privacy, and I don't particularly want to look at all the other neighbors when I sit outside. You know I'm not that neighborly. Out of the three homes, I'm leaning toward the L-shaped, Prairie-style home."

Everett turned and looked at me. "Why do you want to buy a house with an unfinished basement? It doesn't make sense. Spend the money and get a house with everything you want."

"Babe, you're absolutely right. I intend to buy the house I want. We looked at several on Zillow, chose three, and I like the Prairie-style home the best. The basement isn't a priority. I can deal with it later."

"Okay, babe, it's your decision," Everett said with a shrug of his shoulders.

Noting the slight look of disappointment on his face, I wondered why he was making such a big deal out of it. Yes, the home was stunning, but it didn't fit my personality, and I hated that it offered no privacy. I certainly wasn't going to buy a house to suit him. As far as I was concerned, if he liked it that much, he could have offered to buy it for us.

I eventually settled on the two-story Prairie-style home in a quiet neighborhood with less than a thirty-minute drive from downtown in normal traffic. The house had every-thing I required, and the location was perfect. I could walk to public transportation or drive to work. My career was on track, and when I signed the contract on the home, I hoped it would be a home Everett and I would soon share.

Our relationship was in full bloom, and the uniqueness of it was that we rarely argued, which was uncommon in couples. Everett felt that arguing added unnecessary stress and wasn't beneficial in a relationship, so we learned to communicate without hurting or demeaning each other. He also said we'd never go to bed angry. Even when we disagreed, and I was angry or upset, he wouldn't allow it.

In the past, there had been times when I got into bed and turned my back. Everett would lay beside me and say, "I'm not going to let you go to sleep angry."

My anger never lasted even if I tensed up and tried to break his grip. He simply held me tightly and said, "Babe, this will pass."

I sometimes answered, "I know, but not tonight."

Then Everett would say, "Michelle, this isn't how our evening is going to end. I'd hate for something to happen during the night. Then we'll never be able to apologize, and closure will become an endless nightmare."

Hearing his reminder about the fragility of life and that it can be taken at any given time, I'd relax my body, let my anger fade, and fold into his arms.

Although I had to work during Everett's visit, we managed

to check out a couple of museums and took a guided Segway tour of Chicago. Riding a Segway was quite the experience as neither of us had ever ridden one. It was hilarious because it took a moment for me to get my balance. While riding it, I had a flashback to my childhood when I rode double with my sister on her bike. When she hit a curb, I flew off, busted my lip, chipped my front tooth, cried, and walked home with a bloody mouth. I prayed I wouldn't fall off the Segway, as it would be embarrassing, and I damn sure didn't want to bust my lip. Ultimately, we had a great time riding them.

Toward the end of Everett's two-week visit, we both dreaded saying goodbye. The day before his departure, we decided to go out to dinner.

"Babe, I know you enjoy a good steak, so I googled restaurants and discovered that Chicago Cut Steakhouse had good reviews. I made reservations and requested outdoor seating as the restaurant overlooks the Chicago River."

"That sounds wonderful!" Everett said with a wink. "You know how much I love a juicy, tender steak."

I laughed. "I certainly do. In fact, if you're still hungry after dinner, I've got something very juicy and tender for you to nibble on."

"Hmmm ..." he murmured. "With what you're wearing, we might not make it to the restaurant. I sometimes like dessert before dinner." He nuzzled my neck.

For our last evening, my goal was to have Everett's eyes only on me. I wanted to look stunning and sexy, so I wore a backless floral maxi dress with a plunging V-neck exposing a tasteful amount of cleavage, brown platform wedge sandals, and accessorized with gold and silver boho looped earrings and bangles. I pinned my hair in a ponytail to reveal my toned upper body.

"Then why don't I give you a taste? No hands, mouth only."

I pulled Everett close to my chest, slightly pulled open the front of my dress, and allowed him to sample dessert. As he sucked and licked my breasts, I moaned in pleasure. I struggled to pull away from him because I knew if we didn't stop, Everett would be having a different kind of feast.

"Wow, Michelle, you're full of surprises," he whispered. "What's next?"

Laughing, I said. "Dinner."

"Can I have an extra portion?" he asked. "My sweet tooth hasn't been quite satisfied."

"No more, babe! I don't want to spoil your appetite." I gave him a long once-over. "By the way, you look quite handsome this evening."

"Thanks, babe. And you certainly look delicious."

Everett's look was more casual. He stepped out in a black lapel pullover shirt with checkered black and gray slacks, black shoes, and a silver Movado watch. I had no doubt this evening would be special and romantic. To memorialize the evening, we took pictures together in the living room and then went to the balcony to admire the dazzling city lights. As we stood holding hands, we felt transported to a special place that silenced the relentless pulse of the city.

"Michelle, you know much I adore you?" Everett said, turning to me.

"I know. I feel the same."

"These two weeks have been the best of my life," he said. "I feel so close to you. It's like I can finally ..."

I suddenly felt uneasy. "Can what, Everett?" I asked.

He turned to me with a sublime smile. "The purest of love is knowing that true acceptance of someone allows them the freedom to live their life authentically without fear or judgment."

When he spoke those words, the look in his eyes shifted from joy to a plea for understanding. But an understanding of what? Confused, unsure how to respond, I hesitated.

I calmed myself, gazed into his eyes, and gently kissed him. "Luv, freedom isn't living in the shadows. Freedom is being true to yourself."

We silently embraced and stood there for a few more minutes staring at the stars.

"Babe, our reservation is at seven, so we must leave soon."

"Okay," Everett said. "I just need to hit the joint before we go. Do you want some?"

"Sure."

He walked into the kitchen and relit the joint we smoked earlier in the day. He took a couple of deep drags and passed it to me. While I took a drag, I couldn't help but think about what he said.

Chapter Eighteen

After Everett and I left the apartment, a swirl of emotions engulfed me. As we walked hand-in-hand toward the elevators, I thought of the emotion he displayed on the balcony. At one point, he appeared cheerful, melancholy, vulnerable, and unsure of himself. I've never doubted his commitment to me, but while I tried to push his words out of my head, his words circled in my mind like a record endlessly replaying. Although Everett's grip felt strong and reassuring, I still wondered.

Please, Lord, let his love be true and authentic! While we waited for the elevator, I said, "Everett, I'm so glad you came to visit. I've loved every moment of our time together."

He drew me close. "Babe, these two weeks have been like a dream. It felt like we were the only two people in the world. You've filled my soul with love and banished the darkness from my heart."

When Everett said darkness, I didn't want to appear sad, but I felt his emotion and wondered if there were secrets he wanted to share but feared judgment. I turned toward him, cupped his face, and kissed him with tenderness and passion. All I wanted was to stay in this moment with the man I'd fallen in love with. I wanted to reassure him that acceptance was within his reach and that there was no need to fear.

"Babe, tonight we'll celebrate our love, cherish life, and put the past behind us," I murmured.

"Absolutely," Everett said.

~

On the elevator ride down, Everett sighed and looked over at me. "Babe, it's a beautiful evening, but it's Friday, and driving will be chaos. Why don't I order an Uber?"

Hesitantly, I agreed. "Okay, but you should have ordered before we left the apartment."

"I know. You're right. It's just that my mind has been a whirlwind. I hate the traffic here and don't want to spoil the evening by complaining."

"Then you'd better call now. It's 6:00, and our reservation is for seven. Hopefully, there's an available Uber."

"Babe, don't worry." He took out his cellphone. "I got this. If nothing's available, you can drive. I know how much you love it!"

"You're quite the comedian," I said sarcastically as he placed the order.

A few moments later, he gave me a thumbs up. "Uber confirmed. Should be here in ten minutes."

~

As we walked out of my building, I realized Everett was right. The evening was for lovers. It was cool with a light breeze. Music and laughter resonated from the bar across the street and filled the air with contagious energy. People bustled around us, and the city blazed with light and motion. Everett and I swayed to the music as we waited for the Uber.

With traffic congested, as usual, I was glad we could relax on the thirty-minute drive to the restaurant. I enjoyed the jazz the driver played and the refreshing breeze flowing from the driver's sunroof.

When the driver dropped us off a short distance from the restaurant, we noticed a few people on the sidewalk listening to a man playing Bésame Mucho on the guitar. I knew that song because it was an Andrea Bocelli song. The romantic song set the perfect mood for the evening as I wanted Everett to bésame mucho, kiss me a lot, all over my body. We listened for a moment, then Everett dropped a few dollars into the guitarist's money hat before we proceeded to the restaurant.

As we entered the restaurant, a blend of instrumental restaurant jazz softly played. We were impressed with the décor. Soft earth tones added a touch of sophistication to the room and the dim lighting inspired romance. But it was the delicious aroma of food that stirred my appetite. I sat on a nearby bench while Everett checked in with the hostess.

A few minutes after seven, the hostess, a young Black woman, approached. Everything about her, from her short, tapered Afro and figure-hugging blue dress, emanated confidence. She approached and said, "Good evening Mr. James. I'd like to welcome you and your guest to Chicago Cut Steakhouse. Please follow me. Your table is ready."

I couldn't help but notice Everett's eyes on her as she led us to our table. It slightly bothered me, and while I knew I should have ignored it, I couldn't dismiss how I felt. She directed us to an outside table that offered a breathtaking view of the Chicago River.

She handed us the menus and smiled. "Your servers will be with you shortly. Again, welcome to Chicago Cut, and enjoy your evening."

From the corner of my eye, I noticed Everett's eyes glued to her ass. Really, Michelle? You have to admit she's an attractive woman. If that was an attractive man, wouldn't you look? Have you forgotten how you look at Richard?

I shifted my focus from the hostess and watched the boats cruising down the river. I was awed by the gorgeous display of lights from the surrounding buildings that danced on the rippling water.

"Babe, I think we got the best seats in the house," I said with a grin.

"Isn't it spectacular?" Everett asked. "Just the way I want to remember this evening."

As we talked, a young man and woman dressed in white shirts, black vests, black pants, and white aprons approached the table.

"Good evening. Welcome to Chicago Cut. My name is Tina, and this is Maurice. We'll be your servers this evening. Is this your first time dining with us?"

"It is," Everett replied.

"Well, then you're both in for a treat. The food here is exquisite. Have you had time to review the menu?" Maurice asked.

"Not yet. We've been admiring the view," Everett said.

Maurice nodded. "Amazing, isn't it? I never get tired of it,"

"We'll give you a few more minutes to review the menu," Tina said.

~

While we browsed the menu, Tina brought water and a bread basket. A couple of minutes later, Maurice returned.

"Have you decided?" he asked.

"Yes," Everett said. "Let's start with two glasses of the Riesling White. For the appetizer, I'll have the East Coast oysters, and my lady will have the five-piece jumbo shrimp cocktail."

"Excellent choice," Maurice said and left to put in our order.

A couple of minutes later, Tina returned with the wine. "Your appetizers will be here shortly."

"Thank you," Everett said. He picked up his glass. "To the joy in my life, may our happiness continue to flow as endlessly as the universe."

My heart overflowed with joy. Blinking away tears of happiness, I raised my glass. "To us," I said as we clinked our glasses.

When Maurice returned with the appetizers, my eyes lit up. The colorful arrangement of the food looked absolutely amazing.

Everett chuckled. "Babe, don't be shy. Go ahead and eat."

"First of all, you know I'm not shy," I said with a smile. "I just wanted to allow you to get what you wanted first, as I planned to eat the rest!"

"Well, I appreciate your generosity!"

We both laughed and dove in. The shrimp cocktail and oysters were absolutely delicious and so succulent. If I hadn't been in such an upscale environment, I would have licked the plate.

When we finished, Tina and Maurice returned to our table. Maurice cleared away the plates and walked away.

"Have you decided on your entrées?" Tina asked.

"Yes," Everett replied. "I'll have the Signature filet mignon topped with roasted bone marrow, sautéed mushrooms, and whipped mash potatoes, and the lady will have the Chilean sea bass over spinach with a Caesar salad."

"Excellent choice," Tina nodded. "How would you like your steak cooked?"

"Medium rare," Everett said.

When our meals arrived, it was quite evident that the restaurant employed a top-rated chef since the food was lavishly prepared. As we ate, it conjured up sweet memories of home-cooked meals.

"This taste amazing," I raved. "It reminds me of my Sunday dinners growing up."

"What were they like?" Everett asked.

I smiled at the memory. "Before church, my mom seasoned a roast and cut up potatoes and carrots. She put the potatoes and carrots in the refrigerator and slow-cooked the roast in the oven. When we arrived home after church, the aroma in the house was almost narcotic. She knew we'd be hungry and didn't want us begging for a snack. While she finished preparing dinner, Cheri and I set the table. Afterward, my mom beautifully arranged the roast with the side dishes, freshly baked dinner rolls, and salad. If we ate everything, she either served apple pie or German chocolate cake. Not to brag, but my mom is an amazing cook! We always enjoyed a good conversation that sparked a debate. As we ate our dessert, my parents quizzed us with math problems and any other subject they could think of."

Everett grinned. "I feel like I was there. I also have wonderful memories of those Sunday meals my mom prepared. She made killer fried chicken with mashed potatoes, green beans, gravy, and sweet iced tea. The sweeter, the better. The difference was that she prepared our plates, and we went to eat and watch TV in the family room." He took a sip of wine. "My sister, Carla, and I ensured we didn't make a mess because we didn't want to eat at the kitchen table. Hopefully, one day, I can sample your mom's cooking, and you can sample my mom's cooking."

"That would be lovely!" I grinned. "Let's make it happen soon."

We continued to compare home-cooked meals. As we talked and laughed, Everett looked around and made eye contact with Maurice.

Maurice approached and asked, "Can I help you?"

Everett's eyes lingered on Maurice. "I'd like two shots of Patrón with a lime on the side."

"Patrón?" I asked.

"Yes, this is my last night in Chicago, and we're going to have a good time."

"I'm all in. Let's turn it up!" I said with a laugh.

When Maurice returned shortly after with the Patrón shots, he asked, "Will there be anything else?"

Everett gazed at Maurice. It suddenly struck me that he looked at the waiter the same way he looked at the hostess. Granted, Maurice was a handsome young man with dark hair and striking blue eyes, but Tina was also a pretty redhead. The restaurant obviously chose to hire attractive staff, but something about Everett's behavior seemed odd.

"Not at the moment," he said. "Thanks, Maurice."

When I noticed Everett holding Maurice's gaze a fraction too long, it suddenly hit me. Surely, he wasn't flirting with the waiter. As Maurice walked away, I noticed an unfamiliar look in Everett's eyes. A chill coursed through my body. Was this the dark space he alluded to? Michelle, stop it! Get out of your head. You always do this! You read way too much into what you think men say or how they behave. I was so deep in thought that I didn't hear Everett talking.

"Michelle? Babe? Are you okay? You haven't heard a word I've said."

"Oh! I'm sorry. I was thinking about how incredible this evening has been."

"Well, let's make it more memorable and have our shots," Everett said.

We tapped the table with our glasses, took the shots, and chased them with the lime.

"Whoa!" I said, shaking my head. "That was great."

"Want another one?" Everett asked.

"Well, since we're not driving, why not?"

Everett waved at Tina and ordered two more shots of Patrón.

"Babe, you couldn't have chosen a better restaurant," Everett said. "Let's come back."

"Absolutely. Tonight, was magical, but being with you was the cherry on the top," I replied.

Maurice quickly appeared and cleared the table. "Did you enjoy your meals?" he asked, looking at Everett.

"Fantastic food, fantastic service!" Everett said.

I watched them closely, but when Tina appeared with our shots, Maurice walked away.

"Will there be anything else?" she asked.

"No," Everett said. Tina placed the bill on the table and left.

Everett and I laughed, took the shots, and laughed some more. We were lovers. No one or nothing else mattered. Afterward, Everett paid the bill, and we got up to leave. Tina noticed us and came over.

"I hope you had a wonderful evening," she said.

"Memorable," Everett said. "I'd like to thank you and Maurice for providing us with superb service. I'll be sure to leave you an excellent review."

"Thank you. That's our job," she said.

Everett took my hand as we left the restaurant. I felt like a feather drifting on the breeze and didn't want the evening to end.

"Babe, since I'm leaving tomorrow, is it cool if we go straight home? I want you all to myself with no distractions."

I gazed into his eyes. All I wanted to do at that moment was get home and spend the rest of the evening in Everett's arms.

"I'll order an Uber," I said.

Thirty minutes later, we arrived at the apartment. Before we could open the door, Everett pressed me up against it. He passionately kissed me and rubbed my breast. I thought about what the neighbors might think if they saw us, but my concerns evaporated as his lips trailed around both breasts. I felt like my legs wouldn't support my weight. Reaching down, Everett pulled up my dress and slipped his hand into my panties. I damn near screamed from excitement as his fingers slithered inside me.

Breathlessly, I whispered, "Everett, babe, please, oh my God, please…"

He whispered, "Please, what, my love?"

I moaned, "Please open the door. I can't take it anymore…"

Before I could utter another word, Everett's fingers plunged deeper inside. I was so wet I felt it drip onto my thighs. Everett opened the door, and I slumped into his arms. The release left me as limp as a rag doll. He gently picked me up and carried me into the bedroom.

"Oh, I'm not done with you yet," he taunted.

Chapter Nineteen

When I rolled over in bed the next morning, Everett was still asleep. I quietly slid out of bed and went to the bathroom to complete my morning routine. When I returned, I sat down on the edge of the bed near Everett, kissed him on the cheek, and said, "Babe, wake up. Your flight leaves at 12:45, and it's 7:30."

He sleepily turned over and said, "Okay, wake me in thirty minutes."

"Okay."

Thirty minutes later, I returned to the sound of snoring. I watched him for a few moments before I leaned down to caress his face. "Babe, it's time to get up."

Everett stirred and opened his eyes. It warmed my heart to see the smile on his face when he saw me. He motioned me to sit beside him and pulled me into an embrace.

"I'm not ready to leave. I'm going to miss you."

"Same here," I said, tracing my finger along his lips. "I wish you could stay longer."

"We'll be together permanently very soon. Now that you've bought a place, I'll start looking for a job."

I slightly pulled back, looked him in the eyes, and said,

"So, it's actually going to happen. You're going to relocate?"

"Yes, as soon as I secure a job."

A wave of emotion engulfed me, and for a moment, I couldn't speak.

"This is what I've dreamt of for so long!" I gushed. "I love you so much, Everett."

He pulled me closer. "One more time for the road?" he whispered.

I wrinkled my nose. "As long as you take care of your morning breath."

"Oh, it's like that, is it?" he said with a grin.

"Babe, I love you but not your breath ..."

Everett got up and went to the bathroom. When he returned, he took me in his arms, and we created another magical moment.

After I dropped Everett off at the airport, the drive home was chaotic due to bumper-to-bumper traffic. I noticed a Dunkin' Donuts sign while I drove. I've always enjoyed warm glazed donuts, so I figured, why not take the exit? I despised that it was Saturday because it meant I'd be alone for the rest of the weekend. I pulled up to the drive-thru, ordered four donuts and a cup of coffee, and drove home with a donut in my mouth. When I arrived home to the silence, I sat at the kitchen table with my goodies, worked on my laptop for a couple of hours, cleaned up the apartment, and waited for Everett to text me when he got home. As I waited, I thought about our Friday evening lovemaking session.

That night, he and I connected on a spiritual level that I'd never experienced with any other man sexually. Our bodies joined as one in perfect rhythm. Our lovemaking was so intense that Everett said, "Babe, no other woman has ever made me feel like crying. I don't know what's going on." As I daydreamed, my phone buzzed. I picked it up and saw a text from Everett letting me know he had just landed. I texted back, Sounds good. Call me when you get home.

~

Three hours passed, and I had yet to hear from Everett. I called him, but he didn't answer after several rings. I hung up and texted him, Hey, babe, are you home? Call me.

If the flight left at 12:45 p.m., and the flight time was less than 1.5 hours, he should have gotten home around 4ish. I was starting to get concerned when Everett finally called.

He whispered. "Hey, babe, sorry for not calling. I was so tired when I got home. I fell asleep on the couch."

Irritation prickled me. It was the same story he told me after his last business trip. Rather than going with my feelings, I merely said, "I understand. We did have a late night and didn't get much sleep."

"I'm still tired," he yawned. "I need to rest for a couple more hours."

"You're too tired even for a quick chat?" I asked.

He paused. "I've been gone for two weeks, babe. I need to shower and prepare for work next week. I want to get as much done as possible this evening because tomorrow is Sunday, and I want to relax."

Was this the same man I dropped off at the airport that morning? Everett's tone was distant, but it wasn't like he'd flown from Tokyo.

"Okay," I reluctantly replied. "Let's FaceTime before you go to bed."

"Sure, I'll call you." He abruptly hung up.

What the fuck! I know he didn't just hang up on me! I stared at the phone. I desperately wanted to believe Everett was being honest and that there was no reason for him to lie. We'd spent the most wonderful two weeks together; why would he lie? Now I was getting angry. Why did I continually allow the specter of past relationships to influence me so negatively? It was almost like self-sabotage. Although I tried to silence the voices chattering in my head, I couldn't.

What was behind his hot and cold behavior? Wasn't I enough for him? Did he need more? Once again, I questioned my self-worth and conjured up imaginary scenarios of infidelity. Michelle, stop being so paranoid! Stop thinking that Everett's always lying! Just stop it! After I had stressed over him for hours, he called, and we had a wonderful conversation. I knew I needed to control my emotions, but it was difficult to ignore the emotional baggage of past relationships.

Everett and I managed to maintain our long-distance relationship for over six months without drama. We arranged our schedules to ensure we met twice a month. He either flew to Chicago, or I flew to Cincinnati.

During one phone call, Everett said, "Michelle, it's your turn to visit."

I replied, "I know, but unfortunately, I can't come as I have to go on a business trip."

"Can you postpone the trip?"

"No, I'm going with my boss, Janelle."

"Can you come afterward?"

"Not sure. We're super busy at work, but I'll try and work something out."

Everett sounded genuinely disappointed. I thought a

surprise trip would lift his spirits, so after my business trip, I informed Janelle that I was taking a few days off. I booked a flight and flew home to Everett with a sense of excitement and anticipation.

Unfortunately, I was the one surprised. When I got to his house and let myself in, the smell of marijuana greeted me at the door. Immediately, I knew something was wrong, as Everett rarely smoked when we weren't together. Angrily, I stormed into the kitchen and discovered he'd had company. Stunned, I could only stare in disbelief. The trash can overflowed with empty beer bottles, dirty dishes were piled in the sink, the counter was covered with several marijuana pipes and a hookah, and uneaten breakfast was on the stove. I'd never seen the kitchen in such a mess. This definitely wasn't the Everett I knew!

I felt angry, confused, and upset. What the hell was going on? Who was this man I was in love with? Trying to remain calm and not destroy Everett's home, I called him and made up a lie.

He promptly answered. "Hi, babe, what's up?"

"I sent a package that requires your signature. It's supposed to get there around 2:00 p.m. Will you be home?"

"Yes, I'm at the supermarket. I have one more errand to run, and then I'm going home. What did you send me?"

"I can't tell you! Just be there to sign for the package."

"I will. I'll call you when I get back."

"Okay, chat soon."

While I waited for Everett to come home, I moved my rental car two houses down from his house. I quickly walked back into the house, into his bedroom, and damn near vomited when I saw the blood-stained sheets. Nasty ass bastard! He fucked a bitch on her period! As I waited impatiently, I looked around the house and noticed he'd also fucked the bitch in the guest room, but the smell was quite musty. I spotted an unfamiliar suitcase in the corner, but just as I reached for it, I heard the garage door open. I hurried downstairs and waited at the base of the stairs. The shock on Everett's face, when he walked into the house, said it all.

"Michelle!" he cried. "What are you doing here?"

"Well, you pretended you were disappointed when I told you I couldn't come to visit, so I thought I'd surprise you." I was surprised at how calm I was. I thought I'd be yelling, but I was working on autopilot. "You were clearly lying, so let's lay everything on the table right now! How long have you been cheating on me?"

He stared at me. "What?"

"Are you deaf now too? You heard what I said! Why the hell didn't you just tell me? Why the games? Who is she?"

"I'll . . . I'll . . . explain everything," Everett stammered, his face ashen. "I just need to leave for a while."

"What the fuck! Where do you think you're going?"

Then the asshole calmly said, "I dropped her off at the beauty salon."

"What? You've got to be kidding me! You took her to the salon?"

"Look, I'll explain when I get back."

"What do you mean, when you return? We're both going to get her. Let's go!"

I was sure that by now Everett thought I was losing it. Maybe I was! We barely spoke as we got into the car and drove to the beauty salon. On the way, he called and told her I was coming. When we arrived, I couldn't believe my eyes! What the hell? I was shocked when I saw who he'd been spending time with. She was the epitome of a junkie: scrawny, unattractive, with stringy blond hair. My reaction may have been harsh, but it was accurate. Worse, I realized that he would sleep with any woman regardless of her appearance.

Before we picked her up, he told me she had health issues that prevented her from driving, which is why he dropped her off. I could only shake my head and wonder what the hell he saw in this woman. It had to be that she sucked dick damn good!

Everett remained silent as she approached the car.

"Unbelievable," I seethed. "You're cheating on me with that? I can't believe you could be this stupid! What do you see in her? Should I give a fuck that she has health issues?"

The woman got into the back seat, befitting for a slut. It was quiet for a while until she spoke.

"Hi, I'm Ashley. How are you doing?"

I laughed. "Really, bitch? What the fuck! One thing is for damn sure. I'm not your friend. So don't ask me how I am!" Not only was she unattractive, but the bitch reeked of smoke. "Everett, for God's sake, roll down the windows. You're whore stinks."

"I'm not his whore!" the woman yelled. "I'm his girl-friend. I assumed he told you. . ."

Before she finished speaking, I turned around and slapped the bitch across her fucking face and dared her to make a move. I knew I shouldn't have slapped her, but there was no way in hell I'd allow her to yell at me.

She started crying. "Everett, do something! Tell her the truth! You said you told her about me."

Everett remained silent, no doubt because he was scared. He'd never seen me act violently.

"Let me be clear," I retorted, "He hasn't mentioned you to me!"

"He said he told you about me."

"He's been lying to me. Don't think he won't lie to you either!" I cried. "So please enlighten me. What was he supposed to tell me? As you can see, the fool's not talking! Why don't you tell me what I'm supposed to know?"

"Please listen," she pleaded. "He told me you knew about our relationship and weren't a monogamous couple."

I could have punched her. I turned around. "Really? That's what he said? Well, he didn't tell me. Furthermore, you knew he was in a relationship, and you didn't care. It's one thing if you didn't know, but you had the audacity to get in this car all bold and arrogant." I pointed at her with hatred in my eyes. "Oh, okay, now you're playing stupid. You knew what the fuck you were doing!"

I turned to Everett. "Where the hell are we going?"

"I'm taking her home."

"Then you better put some speed on this!"

I should have reached over and slapped the shit out of Everett, but instead, I attacked the woman. Yes, she knew he was in a relationship, but he willingly opened the door and let her into our lives. She went on to tell me every-thing Everett promised her. It was obvious he'd been lying to her for months.

She said, "He told me he wasn't happy with you and had no plans to relocate."

"Oh, interesting! Is there anything else you want to tell me?"

"And he said he was bored with you and wasn't physi-cally attracted to you."

"Wow, okay. So that's what the asshole said."

"Plus, I'm with him all the time." She looked pleadingly

at Everett, who continued to stare straight ahead. "Everett, tell her the truth!"

"Yes, Everett, do tell the truth!"

"He promised me . . . I love him. He said you'd understand."

"Understand what? Look, this conversation is over. My advice to you is to shut the fuck up!"

Throughout the conversation, Everett continued to sit like a mannequin. The woman claimed to be in love with him, and I saw the genuine disappointment in her eyes. I realized she was telling the truth because he'd manipulated her with his lies, and she thought she'd hit the jackpot.

"Michelle, listen. I'm telling you the truth!" she pleaded.

"Don't call me Michelle! You and I aren't friends. I don't give a rat's ass about your truth. You knew he was in a relationship! Did you even consider me? Of course not!"

"You're not even willing to listen to me?" she asked.

"Hell, no, not anymore!"

"Well, did he tell you about Phoenix?" she asked.

"Just shut the fuck up!" Everett shouted. "Don't you start lying to hurt me! It's over between us!"

"Everett, please, please tell her the truth. I love you! Don't do this!"

For a brief moment, I felt sorry for her, but my sympathy didn't last long. She was aware that Everett was in a relationship and didn't care or think about me or what I was dealing with emotionally with him. She fell for his nonsense, and she only had herself to blame. Why should I give a damn about her and the pain she was experiencing? This woman was beneath me. I was in the front seat. She was trash, and he'd just pissed on her dreams.

～

When Everett pulled up to her condo, he got out of the car, grabbed her things, and walked her to the door. I watched as they stood there talking. She was crying hysterically, and from the distance between them, I saw that he was trying to explain. I didn't know what he said and didn't care. I knew it was wrong to admit, but I was glad he destroyed her emotionally. What goes around comes around, and life just slapped her in the fucking face.

When Everett returned to the car, I looked at him and burst into laughter. Was I crazy, or was my brain about to short-circuit? Honestly, I couldn't figure it out. Did the laughter prevent me from killing him? I just didn't know. Why was I sitting beside this liar? Maybe I was in a state of shock, or it was a dream because no sane person would be this calm. I'd seen the ugly side of Everett. He drove and acted like nothing had happened, that this was the norm. He even had the nerve to reach over and take my hand as if to say he was sorry.

I immediately snatched my hand from his and yelled, "Don't ever touch me again!"

He was a heartless manipulator! He didn't even own up to his comments about me when the woman asked him to confirm. He just sat there like a statue. I should have jumped out of the car, run, and not looked back.

~

like her didn't know the meaning of real relationships or how to maintain them. Women like her lacked integrity and self-worth and, for damn sure, didn't have any morals. Mirror, while I'm tired of women like her, I question myself. Why do I continually end up with men like him? Why is it so difficult for me to escape men who repeatedly demonstrate that I'm not enough for them? I wanted to let go. I wanted to move on, but I couldn't. I was trapped in this spider's web of infidelity, mistrust, and the illusion of happiness.

Chapter Twenty

When we arrived at Everett's house, I immediately got into my rental car and left. I needed time away from him to process my thoughts. I drove to a nearby park and sobbed into my hands. I didn't care who saw me. I only needed to release the pain and hurt. The man I loved had betrayed me, disregarded my feelings, and made me feel insignificant. Had our relationship been one big façade? Had I been fooled once again by my illusions of love? I desperately needed someone to talk to but couldn't call my mother or sister because I wasn't in the frame of mind for a lecture, so I called Jennifer.

"Hey Michelle, what's up?" she asked.

Before I could respond, I burst into tears.

"Michelle, what's wrong? Talk to me!"

Sobbing hysterically, I said, "I caught Everett with another woman!"

"What the hell? Where are you?"

"I'm in Cincinnati. I came back to surprise him."

"Where are you now?"

"I'm at a park."

"A park!"

"Yes, a park. I couldn't stand to be around him, so I left."

"Hang up. I'm calling you on WhatsApp so we can video chat."

"Okay."

I hung up. Moments later, Jennifer's photo appeared on WhatsApp.

"Okay," she said soothingly. "Calm down! I'm here for you. Do you want me to come down? I have no problem flying out first thing in the morning."

"No, don't do that. That's too expensive. I'm just happy to talk." My breath caught. Fighting back the tears, I took a couple of deep breaths to calm myself.

"You, okay?" Jennifer asked.

"I don't know what that means," I said. "I feel so betrayed."

"What happened?"

"Jennifer, I can't go into details. I can barely believe it myself. I don't know what to do." I sighed. "I took a few days off work, and now this. I thought he loved me! He said he loved me!"

"Michelle, you know that shit that comes from men's mouths," Jennifer said. "Why don't you come here and stay with me for a few days?"

The thought was tempting, but reality snapped in. I took another deep breath. "I can't. I'm really swamped at work, and I can't take any more time off. I have to be back at work on Tuesday."

"Okay, then stay at a hotel. Don't go back to his place. It's best if you have time to process all this. Will you promise me?"

I shook my head and stared into the distance. "Jennifer, I don't know what to do. Regardless of what happened, I still love him."

"I get it, sweetie. But you need time to think, and returning to Everett isn't a good idea right now."

"I know. I'm just so tired of this. I want to be happy for a change." I stared at a young couple in a passing car. "Is that too much to ask?"

"No, it's not. I need you to listen to me." Jennifer said. "We've always been there for each other in the past and have left it up to each other to accept advice or not. This time, I insist that you go to a hotel. You're hurt and angry. If you go back to Everett, you'll listen to his lies and forgive him. I know you. This time, please put yourself and not your emotions first."

"Okay, okay, Jennifer. I'll call you when I check in."

"Promise me."

"I promise."

After I hung up, I went for a walk. I needed to clear my head. I was experiencing an emotional landslide and felt ashamed, angry, and anxious. I felt like I was on the verge of a nervous breakdown, but after a few minutes, the lushness of the trees and the sound of birdsong soothed me. As I walked, my phone vibrated in my pocket. I retrieved it and saw that Everett was calling. I knew if I didn't answer, I'd regret not expressing myself. With trembling hands, I swiped up on my cell and answered the call.

"Yes?" I could barely contain my anger.

"Where are you?" I heard the concern in his voice.

"What difference does it make where I am? Why do you care? What the hell do you want anyway?"

"Michelle, we need to talk. Please come home."

"Talk about what? You cheated on me!" I shouted.

"Babe, where are you? It's getting late. Just come home."

"I can't! I need some time. . ."

"Babe, please listen to me. I love you. Just come home, and let me explain."

"Explain what! That you're a lying, cheating asshole? You think I'm going to fall for some bullshit fairytale?"

"Okay. Calm down!"

I wiped the tears from my face. "Don't tell me to calm down! I have every right to be upset. How can you say you love me after what you did?"

"Babe, please listen to me. If you don't want to come home, at least tell me where you are, and I'll come to you."

"Enough, Everett! I need time to think."

Hearing him tell me that he loved me weakened my resolve. I knew I should have taken Jennifer's advice, but I needed answers, so I returned to the house.

When I arrived, Everett met me at the door. As soon as I saw his face, I burst into tears. He embraced me and whispered, "Babe, I'm so sorry for hurting you."

I sobbed against his chest. Emotions swirled through me, and I couldn't entirely ignore Jennifer's voice. I knew she'd be furious if she knew I was here.

"No, you're not. If you were, then you wouldn't have done this to us, especially after all that we've been through."

"Babe, please come inside. Let's not have this discussion out here."

Everett guided me inside. As we walked toward the living room, I noticed he'd cleaned up the kitchen. I was so drained that I collapsed onto the sectional. He sat down beside me.

"Did you eat anything?" he asked.

"No."

"I ordered some food. Do you want some?"

"No! I'm not hungry. What I want is the truth! Why the games?" I looked him in the eyes. "Without hesitation, I gave you my heart, and what did you do? You slept with another woman! Oh, and who's Phoenix? Another one of your bitches?"

"There's no Phoenix. She just said that to hurt me because I said it was over between her and me."

"I'm supposed to believe that? You really do have a low opinion of me, don't you!"

"Babe, I'm telling you there's no Phoenix! Why would I even attempt to lie at this point when everything's out in the open?" He threw his hands up in surrender. "I'm telling you the truth. Please, trust me?" He reached for me and tried to lead me to the kitchen. "Come on. You need to eat something."

I angrily shook him off. "Nice try, but you're not distracting me that easily. I'm too exhausted to even think straight!"

"Okay, let's go to bed if you're tired."

I stared at him in disbelief. "Are you serious? You think I'm getting into a bed you shared with your whore?"

"Okay, okay. I'll get you a pillow and blanket."

I paced around until Everett returned with a comforter and two pillows.

"We'll sleep on the sectional."

"Everett, that's not necessary. You can sleep in your room."

"I'm not leaving you."

Too exhausted to fight, I laid down on the sectional. Everett draped the covers over me and sat close to me.

"Michelle, I know I messed up big time. I'm begging you to find it in your heart to forgive me. That woman doesn't mean anything to me."

"She obviously meant enough for you to sleep with her

while she was on her period! Just thinking about what I saw makes me want to vomit. What's wrong with you?"

"Michelle, there's nothing wrong with me. I just messed up. I'm sorry."

"You're only sorry because you got caught! And it's easy to ask me to trust you. How long would this have continued if I didn't catch you? How many more lies? How much more deception? How can I ever trust you again? If you wanted to be with someone else, why didn't you just tell me?" I barely had enough energy for the conversation. I looked the MF square in the face. "Why would you pretend to love me and lie? Why would you even ask me to marry you when obviously that's not what you want!" I yelled.

"I didn't pretend! I do love you, and I want us to get married! I just messed up."

"No, no, you knew *exactly* what you were doing! Again, how long has this been going on?"

"Michelle, does it even matter now? It's over. It's you that I want in my life."

"Really. Yes, it matters!" I threw off the covers and stood up. "You clearly told her about me and our plans for you to relocate, and I'm *certain* you told your whore that you didn't plan on marrying me. It's pretty damned obvious that this has been going on for quite some time."

"Michelle, it hasn't. I'm sorry, can we just move forward? I know it will take time, but I'll do whatever I need to do to regain your trust."

"Trust! You don't even know the meaning of trust. Just stop it, Everett! I can't have this conversation right now. Please leave me alone."

He paused. "Can I at least lay beside you?"

"You got to be kidding me!"

I turned away from him, sat down on the couch, and buried my tear-stained eyes in the cushions. "Do whatever the hell you want."

As I tried to sleep, my phone buzzed. I knew it was Jennifer, so I let the call go to voicemail and texted her. Jennifer, I'm with Everett. Please don't worry. I'll call you soon.

Jennifer texted back. Michelle, we agreed you'd go to a hotel. You promised me. In your emotional state, you know he'll manipulate you as he has in the past. This is a big mistake!

Jennifer, I know you're right. Please try and understand. I need to do this, and I need time to process what has happened. I'll chat with you soon.

"Everything okay?" Everett asked.

"Yes, that was Jennifer checking on me."

"You told her what happened?"

"Yes. I needed someone to talk to."

Everett said nothing and held me close. As we lay together, the tension dissipated, and I relaxed in his arms.

"Michelle?"

"Yes?"

"I need to show you that I love you and that I want us. Can I make love to you?"

As I started to cry, he kissed away my tears. "Why would you do this, Everett? I thought you wanted me to be your wife. Why would you betray me like this? And, no, you can't make love to me. You need to get tested for STDs!"

"Babe, I always wore. . ."

"What? Wore a condom! I doubt that."

I returned to Chicago and didn't pressure Everett to relocate. I continued to move forward with my life and career and didn't put energy into him. Two months later, I purchased my dream home and moved in. Strange as it may have been, I still wanted our relationship. We kept our long-distance relationship going, and surprisingly, we didn't argue during our visits. On one of his visits, he told me he had time to think about our relationship and wanted us.

I initially wanted to question his actions but paused because he seemed to have given it much thought. I prayed he was genuine and evolved beyond his deceit and unfaithfulness. When he told me that he found a job in Chicago and would move in the next five months, I inwardly rejoiced. Considering I had a fully furnished home, Everett decided to sell most of his furniture but kept enough to set up his man cave. He hired a moving company to transport his vehicle and furniture.

This was what I wanted, and I was finally getting my wish. Then, in the background, the faint calling of the Mirror.

Yes, Mirror, what is it that you seek? It's not what I seek. It's what do you seek? Don't worry. I'll approach life's intersection with caution.

When Everett sent me his travel itinerary, I was overcome with joy and called Jennifer.

"Hi, Michelle. It's about time. I was beginning to worry."

"I'm sorry. I know I should have called you sooner. I just needed time to think."

"Girl, no problem. What's going on?"

Pausing, I said, "Well, Everett and I are still together, and he'll be moving here in a few months."

Jennifer sighed. "Michelle, you've been down this road before. Are you certain this is what you want?"

"Jennifer, I know my track record for relationships is terrible, but it's different this time. He's different. He's more attentive and finally putting me first. This is why I needed time to think. I didn't want outside influences to affect my decision. Do you understand?"

"Michelle, it doesn't matter if I understand. All that matter is your happiness."

"Jennifer, thanks for being such a good friend. I love you, and I'll keep you in the loop."

"You better! If he messes up again, you better believe I'm coming there to kick his ass."

Laughing, I said, "I know you will. Chat later."

"Love you, Michelle."

The week before Everett's arrival, I cleaned, shopped, and cleared space in the basement of my home for his belongings. He arrived at the airport on a Saturday afternoon and greeted me with a hug and kiss that would have ignited a flame. On the drive from the airport, I could barely contain my excitement as we drove home. When we got back, I didn't expect him to carry me over the threshold of the front door.

He gazed at me and said, "This is our new beginning."

My heart melted with joy. It was finally happening. I was now with my man in our home. What more could I have wished for?

Unfortunately, my excitement didn't last long.

About five months after Everett moved in, we argued when he wanted me to meet one of his female friends who was coming into town on business.

We were sitting outside on the patio with our usual wine and weed, and unexpectedly he said, "Michelle, a friend of mine will be here this weekend and would like to meet for dinner."

"What are you talking about?" I asked. "You just moved here. What friend?"

"A co-worker from my previous job. She'll be in town for business and reached out to me. I thought it would be nice if we all met for dinner."

"Apparently, you've told her about me."

"She knows I'm in a relationship. She's just a friend."

"Did you agree to the dinner?"

"Yes, I thought it would be okay."

"Everett, I don't know. Don't you think you should have at least mentioned this to me before you agreed?"

"Michelle, it's just dinner and nothing else." He calmly sipped his wine and stared into the yard.

In my heart, I wanted to believe he was telling the truth, so I agreed to the dinner. "Okay, Everett, I'll go with you."

Although I agreed, I became furious when Everett told me the day of the dinner that she'd been to his place.

"Why didn't you tell me she had been to the house?" I asked, struggling to control my frustration. "And why was she there?"

"I had a few people over to the house for dinner, and she came."

"So, you invited her?"

"Yes. As I said, we're just friends."

Knowing that he lied in the past, I assumed there was more to the story. "Everett, we've had our ups and downs. You should have told me sooner. But no, you wait until the day of the dinner. What are you hiding? Everett, the dinner is off!"

"I'm not hiding anything."

"Well, we're not going, and that's final."

He became livid. "It's not right to cancel dinner after agreeing to go!"

"Look, I don't know this woman. And for damn sure, I don't care what she thinks. My advice to you is to cancel the dinner plans."

"Michelle, you're being unreasonable," Everett snapped, pacing around the room. "Nothing is going on with this woman. She's just an ex-co-worker and friend. I think if you meet her, you'll like her."

"You've got to be kidding me!" I stared at him. "So, now you're playing matchmaker? No, not going to happen. As I said, the dinner is off, and you better let her know."

"Look, Michelle, I'm not going to cancel. You just have to trust that I'm telling you the truth."

"Are you serious?" I yelled. "You're going to meet her for dinner?"

Once again, the asshole showed his true colors and left to meet her for dinner. I stood there in disbelief. So much for our new beginning! In a rage, I gathered his belongings, tossed them into his suitcase, sat the bag by the front door, and went to bed.

The next morning, I woke up and discovered Everett had slept in the spare room. I felt like kicking the door open and ordering him out of my house, but my need for an explanation was overwhelming, and truthfully, I didn't want him to leave. I simply walked past his door and went to the kitchen. I made a cup of green tea and went to sit on the patio sofa. As I sat there, I thought there was no way in hell I was going to tell Jennifer about this. I already knew what she'd say, and I wasn't in the frame of mind to hear it.

Eventually, Everett discovered me sitting outside. He sat next to me and took my hand. "I want to be open and honest with you. I know I've let you down in the past, but sometimes I feel as though I'm walking on eggshells, and I'm afraid to tell you what's in my heart. I'm trying, and yes, I'll make mistakes. I need you to believe me when I tell you I'm being truthful."

"Then why did you wait to tell me she'd been to your house?"

"We were trying to rebuild our relationship. I thought about telling you sooner but feared you'd read more into the dinner. Please forgive me for taking you for granted. I really want us."

I looked him in the eye. "The problem, Everett, is that you give me too many reasons to read something into situations. Do you want this relationship, or are you just telling me what you think I want to hear? If you do, you must be transparent and not afraid to talk to me. Otherwise, we're not going to work."

"Babe, I understand. Going forward, I'll do just that. Do you forgive me?"

Sighing, I said, "Yes, I forgive you. Just don't let it happen again."

Mirror, Mirror on the wall, I'm drowning in the sea of fewer possibilities. Day in and day out, without hesitation, I flee from the image that haunts me in the mirror. Judgment waits daily at my feet, and honestly, I don't care what people think. If I concerned myself with the opinion of others, then my life would not be my own, as the opinions of others will take me to darkness where demons rest, and to rest with demons is death. So, please forgive me for my selfishness, for if I'm not selfish, then my road to discovery remains forever distant.

Distant as the Earth is to the sun. I know there's beauty within me, and the beauty that exists is struggling to breathe. My journey is solo and doesn't require an explanation, as self-discovery nurtures independence. How can others know me when their eyes are filled with judgment of my actions? My relationships have taken many wrong detours, and my search for a destination that provides solace is drowned in marijuana and alcohol to repress the claustrophobic shroud that envelops my soul. With every breath, I may fall or stumble, but through it all, I've managed to get back up and start again.

Each time I've gotten up and trusted again, love knocked me down. On my knees with head bowed, I lay with you in my arms. The problem was that love shone brilliantly bright in the daylight and faded into abyssal darkness at midnight. In the darkness, the lover beside me became my worst nightmare. Mirror, was this love at all or just my fear of being afraid to fall, to fall without a safety net? I thought I knew who I was, and I thought I knew what I wanted, but I got trapped in his sadistic game of life. Hopefully, I was not defeated, just delayed.

Chapter Twenty-One

Despite the drama, Everett and I managed to get our relationship back on track, and trust and laughter returned. Even during our troubled relationship, our home life was easygoing, and we never wasted a single moment to make each other feel loved. Our time together was precious, and to foster a tighter connection, we took weekend trips. When it came to our getaways, Everett never asked me to share the cost. He simply gave me his credit card and left the travel arrangements up to me.

I felt safe and secure in the relationship, and Everett never failed to surprise me. One evening, I arrived home before him, and as I prepared dinner, I paused to pour a glass of sparkling Roscato sweet red wine. I picked up my cell, opened the Apple Music app, selected Dave Hollister, and swayed to the beat of the music. As I stood by the sink gazing out the kitchen window, I heard the garage door open. I turned to greet him and was pleasantly surprised when I saw the bouquet of red roses in his hands.

With pure delight and joy in my heart, I said, "Oh, Everett, you're so sweet."

"Babe, for the most caring and beautiful person in my life."

He placed the roses on the counter, kissed me on the forehead, reached for my hand, and led me to the living room. There we danced to Falling in Love Again.

As we danced, Everett whispered, "I love you. Thanks for being patient with me." The man I'd fallen in love with had shown up and was now showing out. He held me, and I rested my head on his chest, wondering how this loving man could want another woman when I gave the best I had to offer. Quite often, in the early stage of a relationship, people were eager to please and do things for each other like laundry, cleaning up, and bringing gifts, etc. Unfortunately, this faded over time. However, when it came to Everett, I genuinely enjoyed doing the expected and unexpected, and he reciprocated.

Finally, our love was in full bloom, and I believed nothing could tear us apart. On one of our weekend trips, Everett suggested a weekend trip to Miami, Florida, to visit his sister, Carla. I booked first-class tickets on American Airlines for the following weekend. During our visit, we decided to go to a nightclub. When we arrived, Everett went to the bar to get drinks. While I spoke with his sister, a woman walking in our direction stumbled. As she reached to grab the nearest table, her drink flew from her hand and smacked me right in the face.

I stood there in disbelief. Did this just happen? As I stood there, I noticed Everett moving rather quickly with our drinks. He sat the drinks on the nearest table and rushed to catch her before she fell.

I screamed. "Don't you see I'm soaked?"

Everett said, "It's just a drink, Michelle. Go to the ladies' room and clean up."

Obviously, he didn't give a damn that the drink had spilled all over me.

Then he began to laugh. "Michelle, you should have seen the look on your face!"

What was fucked up was that he encouraged his sister to laugh. I couldn't believe they both thought it was a joke. His sister didn't even know me, yet she had the fucking nerve to laugh.

I shouted, "Do I look okay? What the hell's so funny? Are both of you crazy?"

I looked at him with hatred in my eyes. Although I wanted to curse them, I chose to walk away. The woman stopped to apologize and accompanied me to the ladies' room.

I couldn't help but wonder what man found pleasure in another person's shame. Of course, that was the end of our evening, and we returned to the hotel.

When we got to our room, Everett asked, "What's wrong with you?"

Unbelievable. "Really? What's wrong with you?" I retorted. "And why on God's green Earth would you ask that stupid ass question? You thought it was funny having a drink tossed in my face?"

And just like a man, he replied, "Michelle, I saw everything. It wasn't intentional. You saw her trip."

I had to calm myself because I was ready to punch him in the face. "No! What I saw was your concern for her, not me. How do you think I felt when I saw you rushing toward her? There were other men around who could have helped her. I was dripping wet, and you totally disregarded my feelings by laughing at me in front of everyone."

Everett still refused to acknowledge that he messed up. He sat on the bed and took off his shoes. "I saw the look on your face, so I laughed to lighten the moment. I didn't want you to get upset."

I shook my head in disbelief. "You didn't want me to get upset? Really? So why the hell did you encourage your sister to laugh?"

Then the fool said, "I just thought it would have lightened the situation."

Anger coursed through my veins. I needed to get out of the room. I knew if I stayed, I would kill the son of a bitch. I walked out. A couple of hours later, I found him sitting on the bed watching TV as though nothing had happened.

I was tired of his games. "Everett, I can't do this anymore. You consistently put other women before me. I've had enough! This relationship is over, and I want you to move out! Tonight, you made me feel and look like a fool! Are you so insecure that you take pleasure in humiliating others to boost your ego?"

"You need to calm down, Michelle," he said. "When you do, then we can talk about it. And for the record, I'm not moving because I came to Chicago to be with you, so it's final."

I stared at him in silence. He might as well have recited his shopping list with all the concerns he showed. I packed my suitcase and went to book a separate room. On the day of our departure, Everett and I met on the plane. I tried to change my seat, but the flight was fully booked. We didn't speak to each other during the flight.

On the drive home from the airport, I still refused to acknowledge him.

"You know, we shouldn't hold onto anger," he said.

It was all I could do to keep from screaming at him.

"Maybe you shouldn't hold onto your inconsiderate and selfish behavior," I snapped.

He had no response, so I turned toward the window and ignored him. I was so glad my annual trip to Sivananda Ashram Yoga Retreat in the Bahamas with Jennifer was approaching because I badly needed time away from him. The trip would allow me to clear my mind and reconnect with my inner self.

In the days before I left for the trip, Everett and I barely spoke to each other. He never apologized for his behavior and insisted that I'd overreacted. I was scheduled to depart Saturday morning for my seven-day trip. Everett was nowhere to be found, so I took an Uber to the airport. After a couple of days away, I decided to call him. Of course, he was unreachable. I left a message. I hoped he would have returned my call, but he didn't.

The realization of Everett's past infidelity began to flood my mind. I knew I told him the relationship was over, but he insisted he wasn't moving. I wondered where he was and why he wouldn't return my calls. Now that I was away, he had the perfect opportunity to find comfort in the arms of another woman.

When I should have been enjoying my time with Jennifer, my imagination was running wild. I repeatedly called him, but he didn't answer. I knew I screamed and cursed Everett, but surely the MF couldn't be so busy that he couldn't answer the phone!

Jennifer noticed my distraction. "Michelle, please don't call him again. You're becoming more agitated with each call, and by now, you know he's not going to answer the phone."

"I know." I glanced at my phone. "I just hoped he'd talk to me."

"I realize this is a difficult time for you, but you must let it go and find peace," Jennifer said with a sigh. "We only have a few more days left on our trip, and you've been miserable for three days. This isn't the kind of getaway that's going to help you, Michelle. You know I love you, but enough is enough. The way that you're behaving is unhealthy. We came here to relax and spend quality time together, and you're ruining our trip. If you want to sit around and mope over Everett, then you can do that alone." Jennifer got up to leave. "I'm going to the beach. If you want to come, you're more than welcome, but leave the dark energy behind."

Looking at the sadness in Jennifer's eyes, I felt ashamed. "Jennifer, I'm sorry. You're right. This is my issue, not yours. Please forgive my selfishness."

I put my phone away, changed into my bathing suit, and joined Jennifer on the beach. In the three days remaining in the Bahamas, we enjoyed the activities we planned. Being engaged helped me release my stress and negativity energy and reconnect with Mother Earth. The joy that dissipated eventually resurfaced, and I enjoyed my time with Jennifer. After the trip, I felt energized, confident, more present, and most importantly, I loved myself.

When I returned home late Saturday evening from the trip, I discovered a note on the counter that read, Just like you, I needed time away to think. After I read the message, I felt like my heart had been ripped from my chest. Returned home happy, and with one swipe, I'm back in this fucked up reality. I understood that Everett may have needed time to process what happened between us, but why would he toss me aside and not have enough respect to answer my calls? I wanted to call him but suspected he wouldn't answer. So, I grabbed my bags and went to my room. After I showered, I reached into the nightstand, took out a joint, lit it, took several hits, and went to bed.

I woke up the next morning to the sound of barking dogs. I rubbed my eyes and quickly reached for my phone to see if Everett had called or messaged me. Nothing. Before I got out of bed, I tried meditating, but my mind kept going back to Everett. With a heavy heart, I got out of bed, washed my face, and went to the kitchen to make coffee. As I sipped my coffee at the kitchen table, feeling alone and unloved, I thought about my good friend Ryan.

I met Ryan in college. I was a freshman, and he was a senior. I was walking and apparently looked lost. He stopped and asked if I needed help finding whatever I was looking for.

Looking at him, I said, "I'm looking for the admissions office."

Ryan pointed me toward the building. "Let me show you the way."

I paused and thought of the advice my parents gave me before I left for college. "If you just point me in the direction, I can find the building."

"Come on. I'll walk with you. It's okay. There are quite a few people around, so you have nothing to worry about."

Even then, something about Ryan deeply touched me, so I let him show me the way to the building.

As we walked, we briefly discussed what I should expect in my first year. He was kind and non-threatening. I relaxed and enjoyed the walk and conversation. With each passing minute, I felt as though I'd known him for years.

After Ryan walked me to the admissions building, he gave me his cell number and said, "If you need anything, give him a call."

I took his number. "Okay, I will."

As he walked away, I thought, Wow! That was so sweet of him to walk with me.

As time passed, Ryan began to treat me like his little sister and guided me through my first year of college. He warned me of the dangers associated with frat parties and told me it was in my best interest not to attend. He'd say, "Don't be in a rush. Life won't pass you by. Take this first year to learn how to navigate being on your own." We often discussed relationships, goals, and what was expected of me after college. Even after college, we remained in contact with each other. With Ryan, I didn't have to pretend. I could be my authentic self, and even if I tried to act out of character, he called me out on my shit.

I desperately needed a male perspective right now. As I sat thinking about Ryan, I picked up my phone and called him.

"What's this? Michelle Davis?" he said.

I was pleasantly surprised that he answered the phone because I needed to hear a friendly voice.

"Stop playing. You know it's me."

"Well, this is a nice surprise. I haven't heard from you in a while. What's going on?"

Before I could respond, I burst into tears.

"Michelle, what is it?"

"Ryan, I . . . I really need someone to talk to."

"Well, you know you can talk to me. What's going on?"

I took a deep breath. "It's my relationship. It isn't good, and I don't know what to do. My partner cheated on me. I forgave him, but now his behavior is unacceptable. In short, we took a trip to visit his sister in Florida and went to a club. While at the club, a woman tripped, and her drink flew in my face. When he saw what happened, he quickly rushed to help the woman, totally disregarded me, and had the nerve to laugh. He said he laughed because he didn't want me to get upset. Please tell me what man laughs at a person he is supposed to love?"

"Michelle, why did you forgive him, and how soon?"

"Less than a week. I love him, and I want our relationship to work."

"I'm assuming he knows you'll forgive him no matter what he does. It's clear he wanted you to feel like you over-reacted in that situation. Have you told him how you felt about the situation?"

"Yes. He said I overacted, so I told him our relationship was over because I was tired of his BS."

"What did he say?"

"He said he moved to Chicago to be with me and wasn't going anywhere."

Ryan exhaled. "Michelle, I know you don't want to hear it, but when you immediately forgave him, that sent the wrong message, and he's exploiting your weakness and love. You need to reevaluate the relationship. If it's unhealthy, you must let it go. If you don't, it's not going to end well."

"Ryan, I've repeatedly tried to disconnect from him, but he's so charismatic and smooth-talking. Before I realize what's happened, I'm back in his trap."

"Michelle, are you certain you want to be in this rela-tionship?"

"Well. . ." I paused. "Sometimes, I'm certain, and then there are times when I'm so confused and struggle with letting go. I want to feel like I'm number one in his life, not second."

"Michelle, I can't tell you what to do. I can only suggest this because it's not my life. It's yours. I can hear the confusion in your voice. I suggest space in the relationship. Space will allow you time to think about what you want from life and your relationship. By no means will it be easy, but it's definitely something that you need to do."

"Ryan, I know you're right." I shook my head. "I just don't know if I have the strength to let go."

"You have the strength. You just need to take the first step."

While I was talking with Ryan, I heard the garage door open.

"Hey, Ryan, my partner just returned. Thanks for listening and being such a good friend. We'll talk later."

"Okay, Michelle. Just know I'm here for you anytime you need to talk. Take care of yourself."

"I will. Thanks again. Got to go for now."

Chapter Twenty-Two

After I finished my call with Ryan, I pretended to clean the kitchen. Everett walked in with his overnight bag and just looked at me. Without a word, I turned and walked out to the patio. Shortly after, Everett came out and sat beside me as if nothing had happened between us. We didn't rehash the drink in my face episode or the note he left on the counter. I was emotionally exhausted and knew an argument would have been unproductive. I realized I should have been firm in asking him to move out, but in some sick, twisted way, I was glad he was home.

I consciously recognized I was in an emotionally draining relationship, and Everett was the jailer who kept the key to my jail cell. He always knew what to say to draw me back into the relationship. He showered me with gifts and made me feel better than I did with anyone else. The deep desire to have his love compromised both my judgment and emotions.

No matter how often I looked in the mirror and saw the unrecognizable, tearful face staring back at me, I didn't want to fight with him or beg for his attention. Nor did I want to compete with other women. I just wanted him to stop behaving like an idiot and recognize that we could have a prosperous future.

∼

Despite our dysfunctional relationship, we remained together for more than five years, and during that time, we often shared many joyous and hilarious moments. I recalled one evening as I sat in bed browsing through a magazine and watching music videos on our TV. Everett came into the bedroom with a drink and a smile on his face just as I Feel Good by James Brown was playing.

He pretended to be James Brown and danced around the room.

Laughing, I said, "That's not the James Brown dance." I jumped out of bed and did my best impression of James Brown. We burst into laughter and fell onto the bed.

Everett turned toward me and asked, "May I?"

I whispered, "Yes, you may."

It was a magical night. We floated on a cloud that showered us with an emotional rain alternating between stormy torrents of sadness and gentle drizzles of tenderness and love. Our love was like a rollercoaster ride filled with sharp twists and turns, leaving us giddy and gasping for breath. Every steep incline or drop often left us reeling with fear or eagerness for the next unseen turn in our relationship. I didn't feel like Everett was taking advantage of me because I consciously chose to let him remain in my life. When it was just us with no outside distractions, I felt safe and found comfort in his arms. He could calm my doubts simply with a kiss on the cheek or a hug that allowed me to touch his soul.

∼

Our relationship consumed my days and nights, and I often prayed we'd both change because peace was a distant shore in my life. I was raised in the church, and with all the uncertainties in my life, I decided to return in the hope of healing my mind, body, and spirit. The church was my avenue of escape as God's Spirit was the warmth of summer's day, infusing me with strength.

As a single woman with no children, I quickly discovered that many women strutting around in their Sunday hats and fancy dresses were merely acting. They didn't view me as a sister but as a threat. It was clear in their behavior when they introduced me to their spouses or partners. Rather than accept me as a sister in Christ, they chose to cast me out or judge me because of their insecurities.

I thought about these women and wondered if they chose men who didn't share their faith. Did they remain firm in their faith, or did they discard it when they married these men? Were they now trying to change them, mold them into a reflection of themselves? Were they so threatened and disturbed by a single woman's mere presence, a woman not even thinking about their men?

To ease the tension, I sat with a scarf over my legs to prevent gossip in the church. As broken as I was, I redirected my thoughts to find comfort in God. One particular Sunday, I must have appeared sad and lost in my thoughts. As I stood fighting tears, a woman approached and placed her hand on my shoulder. "No matter what you're going through, you'll be all right," she said. "Take your eyes off the situation, focus on the greater, and most importantly, don't concern yourself with the thoughts of other people."

The church became a haven where I could connect to a Higher Source. I eventually joined a woman's group, and to my surprise, the members steered away from drama and encouraged us not to measure our disappointments against our possibilities. I never shared what was transpiring in my personal life with them because, in my heart, I knew I wasn't going to leave Everett.

In church, I could disconnect from my current reality, rejoice, and give thanks to the Creator for the blessings bestowed upon me. However, after church, I was forced to accept the lie I was living and the change that would happen when I made an effort. I sincerely wanted to believe Everett when he told me I was the woman he wanted to grow old with, but I always found it difficult to trust his words or my actions.

As I walked into the kitchen early morning on a workday, I noticed Everett's cell on the counter unlocked. It buzzed. I nervously looked around to ensure he wasn't nearby and picked up his phone. I noticed a text from a woman named Kelli that read, If she hasn't you told lately that you're loved, I want you to know I love you. That's all I saw. I was floored. Would Everett ever change? Same old shit on a different day!

At that point, I made it my mission to check his phone. I knew I was invading his privacy, but I didn't care! Thereafter, I often waited for him to fall asleep so I could check his phone. I would pray it was unlocked. I badly wanted to see the conversations he had with these women. I didn't need confirmation of his infidelity. Perhaps I simply wanted to torment myself. Shit! I don't know! I just needed to see the messages!

A week later, I arrived home from work late and discovered Everett in the shower. I looked around the room and saw his cellphone on the nightstand. My heart started hammering as I picked it up. It was unlocked. I listened to make sure Everett was still in the shower. With shaking hands, I quickly scrolled through a few messages. To my surprise, he wasn't only involved with one woman; there were several. He told one woman that he was in an unfulfilling relationship, and with the others, he just toyed with their emotions.

The text I'd previously seen came from a woman who knew he was in a relationship. As I read her message, I discovered they'd been seeing each other for about two weeks. One message read, No matter what you're going through, just know I'm here for the man I love. If you want me, then come and get me. Before I realized it, with his phone in my hand, I stormed toward the bathroom like a cresting tsunami about to destroy everything in its path. I stopped. How could I confront him? I'd gone through his phone. I took a deep breath and tried to calm down.

I felt a sick twisting in my gut. This was more serious than I thought. Was Everett secretly planning to move? Here we were, living together, trying to plan our future, and this scumbag already had another woman. No matter what I did, he didn't appreciate it. I cooked, cleaned, and took damn good care of him, but it was never enough. The question was, would it ever be?

After going through Everett's phone, I was so overcome by resentment and hatred that I had to sit down before I started smashing whatever was within reach. No matter what happened in our relationship, I forgave him every fucking time, and this was my reward. All I wanted was to give him a dose of his own medicine. I wanted revenge! But I had to plan it carefully, not act like a hysterical woman.

As I stood there with Everett's phone in my hand, I heard him turn off the water. I quickly returned it to the nightstand, rushed to the bedroom entrance, and called out, "Hi, babe, I'm home."

He stepped out of the bathroom with a towel wrapped around his waist. He approached, kissed me, and dropped his towel.

I struggled to contain my disgust. Did this MF actually think I was going to suck his dick? If I hadn't gone through his phone, I would have, but not now. If I put his dick in my mouth, I'd be Lorena Bobbitt, except I would have bitten it off.

"Babe, why don't you get on your knees and please me?"

I looked at him and said, "Babe, I just arrived home. I'm tired and don't have the energy."

"Okay, then I'll do the work. Bend over the bed, and let me fuck you." His tone was almost frightening.

"Everett, I said, I'm tired."

"Michelle, you've never turned down a good fuck! What's wrong?"

"Nothing. As I said, I've had a long day, and I'm exhausted. Can I at least freshen up and relax for a few minutes?"

"Okay, Michelle," he said, wrapping the towel around his waist. "Maybe later on?"

Nodding distractedly, I said, "Sure, Everett." I busied myself, changing out of my clothes.

Everett watched me for a few moments. "Babe, on a different topic, my parents plan to visit next weekend."

I almost couldn't wipe the smile from my face. Now I had the opportunity to inflict some real pain!

"Everett, I won't be here when they come," I calmly stated. "I already made plans for that weekend."

"Can't you postpone them?"

"I can't. I'm meeting Jennifer in St. Louis. She already bought her ticket. I'm not canceling on her."

"Really, Michelle? You're visiting Jennifer?"

"Yeah." I rolled my eyes. "Look, Everett, communication between us is almost non-existent. At this point, I don't give a damn about pretending we're the perfect couple."

I felt a twinge of satisfaction at the anger in his eyes.

"Fine!" he said, storming out of the room. "Do whatever the hell you want to do! The one weekend I need you, you disappoint me! I guess I'm definitely not getting my dick sucked tonight!"

~

I barely gave what he said a second thought. It was interesting how he played the guilt card, but then I'd also lied about meeting Jennifer in St. Louis. I just booked a hotel for that weekend in Chicago and spent the time shopping and going to the movies. I wasn't even concerned that Everett might see me in town. What was hilarious was that when I returned, he accused me of cheating!

"Where have you been?" he asked. "I called and texted you all weekend. Why did you ignore me?"

"I didn't ignore your calls," I said matter-of-factly. "I simply didn't feel like talking to you. I needed time to think about this relationship, and I was spending time with Jennifer!"

"Really? You were with Jennifer? I doubt it. If you were, why didn't you answer my calls? So where were you?"

"Everett, what the hell does it matter at this point?" I unpacked my bag and didn't bother looking in his direction. "I don't have the energy for you or this discussion. Think whatever the hell you want!"

"Okay, so it's like that?"

"Yes, it is!"

Everett obviously thought I was a hopeless woman, but in reality, I was a woman with a plan. I never intended to be unfaithful, but when he showed his true colors by disrespecting my feelings, my perspective changed. If he thought I was going to act like a scolded puppy cowering in the corner while he secretly wined and dined other women, he was in for a rude surprise.

I looked beyond the now. For too long, I'd invested my heart, mind, and time in Everett and believed we could evolve past the bullshit. It was a painful lesson to accept that it was all for nothing. He continued to lie and be unfaithful, and foolishly, I played along. I couldn't blame this disastrous relationship on other women. Everett opened the door and welcomed them, calling them "desperate." No wonder he found it easy to cheat.

His dishonesty took a massive physical and mental toll on me. I felt myself slipping into the dark realm of jealousy and doubt and struggled to turn it around. Stupidly, I worried about screwing up a beneficial living arrangement because Everett was paying half of the mortgage and bills, and I had free use of his credit card. But I wasn't going to bother myself with him any longer. If he wanted to cheat, let him. If he wanted to leave, I'd open the door and let him go. Instead of continuing to stress and upset myself, I became Everett.

On one of my business trips, I met one of those guys who looked like he could give you some good wall-to-wall action. He was the fantasy depiction of a cowboy: tall, blond, rugged, and with a toned body that promised a very good ride. He was sitting in the hotel lounge bar, having a beer. I casually walked up to the bar and ordered a drink.

While I waited for my drink, I asked, "Is this seat occupied?"

He turned to me and smiled. "No."

I sat down. "I'm Michelle. How are you this evening?"

"Nice to meet you, Michelle. I'm Lake. So far, I'm having a good evening. Are you attending the conference?"

"No. Job training." I took a sip of my drink.

"Are you here for the week?"

"Yes. What about you?"

"I'm hosting a conference," Lake said. He swirled the ice in his glass. "What are your plans for the evening?"

"No plans. Just chilling out at the bar."

We sat and talked for several hours. During our conversation, I felt like I knew him better than Everett. I thought, Damn! I need some good dick! If I were a man, I knew what I'd do, so I invited him to my room for a nightcap. He accepted, and off we went. For two days after class, we had dinner and dessert, with me as dessert. The last night before we left, he told me that he wanted to see me again, and I felt the same.

I needed the distraction from the void within me. I needed to feel desired, and the time we spent together was amazing. My body ached for more with his every touch. I felt alive because I was alive! If Everett could cheat and come home to lay in the same bed with me, I could do the same and do so without guilt. My Mr. Lounge Man often met me on my other business trips and gave me some intense wall-to-wall, bed-to-floor, and car action. The affair was stimulating, and I enjoyed my taste of the forbidden fruit.

Then came the big letdown. Lake told me he was married. Damn! For a moment, I honestly didn't care. It was so good, all I wanted was more! Then I thought, what the hell was I doing? Had I forgotten how devastated I felt when I looked through Everett's phone? So, I ended the affair and vowed to stick only to single men. I believed that when a woman learns that a man is married or in a relationship, she needed to walk the fuck away and never look back. If she didn't, she needed her ass kicked, figuratively speaking.

Lake was my first, but not my last. There must have been something about me because men noticed, and I wasn't shy. I also discovered younger men desired mature women. My next encounter was with a twenty-six-year-old man I met at the mall, offering a free session to promote his body sculpturing business. He gave me his business card. A month later, I called him and scheduled a session. I met him three times a week at his studio for forty-five minutes of personal training.

I looked forward to seeing his cute smile and hard body. During one of our sessions, he asked if I was in a relationship. My first instinct was to lie, but I decided to be honest.

"Why do you want to know?" I asked.

"I'm interested in getting to know you better."

At first, I thought he was too young, and I hoped he wasn't looking for a sugar mama. No way in hell was I going to pay for his time. I might be older, but I wasn't a fool. However, over time, he became very playful, greeting me with a hug and kiss on the cheek. Was it my walk? Was it my confidence? What did he see? He was so young and yummy with his black dreadlocks pulled up in a man bun. His brown skin glowed in the sunlight, and his colorful tattoos perfectly complemented his enviable muscles. Maybe he just wanted to pleasure an older woman. I didn't know, but I intended to find out.

When Everett was away on business trips, I'd called my boy toy and spent as much time as possible with him. Yes, I knew it was a sexual connection but a damn good one! Thumbs up! He wasn't in a relationship.

Everett was being Everett, and I was enjoying the

company of a younger man. I was finally doing what I wanted, and I didn't care or think about Everett. The affair lasted over six months. But really, what was I doing? Would I need more and more to fill the void in my life? I honestly thought I was emotionally equipped to behave like a man, but I didn't realize I was on the path to destruction. I had to stop, so I ended the relationship with my boy toy and hit the pause button.

Mirror, Mirror on the wall, please catch me before I fall, and wake me up from this dream, for this nightmare of life is mentally taking its toll on me. Desperately, I struggle to reach your lifeline of hope that's daily cast at my feet. I feel as though you can't see me since I've painted my face with truth and lies that have blended into a dark shade of doom and feel as though you've abandoned me. Blinded by the relationship failures in me, the path I travel prevents me from finding my way back to you. Please reassure me that this is not my fault but the fault of the people around me because I'm falling deeper and deeper into the suicidal abyss of a black sea.

Mirror, please stay with me! It is you that needs to save me, save me from the destruction of self. For if you don't save me, then you will bury me. Bury me beneath the sea where my dreams will no longer exist. Mirror, do you hear me? I said I'm drowning, and I don't know what to do! Why do you sit quietly as I scream for you? I can't do this anymore, but I find myself trapped in his web of lies. The more I mentally struggle to escape the manipulation of the puppet master, the greater the penetration of my mind, body, and soul increases. Mirror, I'm too weak to fight when all I want is to be loved, loved by the one who said he loved me.

Frustrated, I shattered my reflection in the Mirror, and the Mirror became quiet.

Chapter Twenty-Three

Deep melancholy lived in my heart. The mirror was quiet and no longer responded to my questions. I kept asking myself, why are you in this relationship? Get the hell out of this mess! He's not going to marry you! You wasted tremendous time with him, and he continuously proved that he doesn't respect you or the relationship. My mind shifted to his conversations with these women. I worried about what they thought of me, and I didn't want other women to have that power over me.

All of them knew he was in a relationship. Then the darker thoughts seeped through. Is what they have between their legs better than what I gave Everett for the past several years? They probably thought I was weak and incapable of satisfying my man. Why was I so focused on these bitches who didn't even give a damn about me? I knew the notion was ridiculous, but I didn't want to lose to another woman. I'd be known as the invisible woman who couldn't keep her man. A failure!

I even thought about women from past generations who had no option but to stay in abusive relationships or close their eyes to infidelity. Yes, the social stigma of divorce was frowned upon and would have been an embarrassment to the family, so most women remained in the marriage and suffered in silence.

~

I recalled when I was growing up, most of the women on my block worked, and, based on what I witnessed in their homes via my friends, they appeared to be content. What I didn't realize until I was much older was that their marriages were filled with resentment and lost years with controlling and unfaithful men. Most of the women had three or more children and undoubtedly felt it was best to remain with their husbands and not jeopardize their home lives.

Having to endure mental and physical abuse most often catapulted these women into closet depression that forced them to hide their truest selves from family and friends and pretend that their home lives were not dysfunctional. I believed the bedroom, without the presence of their husbands, became their safe place. There, they could have quietly cried and found comfort in the calmness of the day. Left in peace in their rooms, they would have looked at themselves in the mirror, seen their strength, and reminded themselves that they had to survive for their children.

These women suffered in silence and faced self-esteem issues, as well as the fear of an uncertain future, things that could have led them to suicide. These women were beaten, abandoned, and threatened with death if they tried to leave their marriages. They endured the wrath of their husbands for their children's sake. Although they attempted to shield their children from the turmoil, they failed to recognize the long-term emotional impact it would have on them. Most often, daughters went on to mirror their mothers' actions, and sons mirrored their fathers' actions. Was I mirroring my mother's actions? I didn't lack confidence. I embraced the unknown, had a stellar career, and was financially secure.

~

In retrospect, I realized I was damaged. I was that little girl that looked at her mother, trying to understand the meanness of my parents.

As a little girl, I often asked my mother, "Do you love Daddy?"

Her response was always yes. She never spoke ill of my father.

Then I asked, "Why do you go to your room and cry? When we called for you, you whispered, 'Please give me a moment?'

My mother failed to see the confusion in my eyes and the fear that engulfed me when my father came home intoxicated. She failed to see me hiding under the bed in fear that he'd beat me as he'd beaten her, and her tears were a hurricane destroying everything in its path, including me. I felt like screaming, "I'm drowning!" but she couldn't hear or see me because she was doing all she could not to drown. She assumed we kids couldn't hear them arguing in the bedroom or her muffled screams after being slapped in the face. Now, I was permitting Everett to slap me repeatedly in the face with his infidelity. I was the woman searching for acceptance in all the wrong places.

Tormented by endless drama and unfaithfulness, I desperately needed help, so I reached out to my spiritual counselor. She knew my deepest secrets and desires and was supportive, understanding, and nonjudgmental. During one of our sessions, she listened and provided guidance but warned that if I continued to involve myself with men at a lower vibration than me, the spirit channel I opened would be difficult to close. I had to change my course of action. I thought I was aware of the dangerous road I was traveling and felt I was equipped to handle the consequences. Well, those consequences finally caught up with me.

One evening, Everett and I had gone out to dinner. During our meal, I became quite nauseous. My hands grew clammy, and I broke out in a cold sweat. He reached over and placed his hand on my shoulder. "Michelle, are you okay?"

"Not really. I feel a little sick. Excuse me. I'm going to the restroom."

"Okay. Let me help you up."

"No, no, that's okay. I'll be right back."

I'd barely left the table when I felt the gorge rising in my throat. I rushed to the restroom, but as I reached for the door, I threw up. I was grateful no one else was there. After I finished, I gathered a few paper towels and cleaned up the mess. I washed my hands and rinsed out my mouth. I still felt shaky, so I waited a few moments before returning to the table.

"What's wrong?" Everett asked.

"Not sure. Maybe it was something I ate. Can we go? I'm not feeling that well."

"Okay, let me take care of the bill."

Over the next couple of days, my symptoms worsened. Finally, I asked Everett to take me to the hospital. When we arrived, I was doubled over from excruciating abdominal pain. The nurse checked me in, took me to a room, and assessed my symptoms. She explained that I was having a miscarriage. I was stunned. How the hell could this be happening?

"Would you like me to get your husband," the nurse asked.

"No!" I said frantically. "He's not my husband!"

I had no desire to share this painful moment with Everett, so, I laid in bed for a few minutes as I struggled to make sense of the trauma I had just experienced. Finally, I dried my tears and asked the nurse to bring him to the room. When Everett arrived, I wanted to tell him the truth because I needed him to comfort me. Instead, I lied and told him I had kidney stones and had to stay in the hospital for several days. In my heart, I sensed he knew I wasn't being truthful, but he didn't ask any questions.

When I returned from the hospital, depression greeted me at the door. It felt like I sank into quicks that suffocated me in the deepest abyss of despair. I looked expressionlessly at Everett and felt a stab of loathing for the agony he brought into my life. All I wanted was marriage and a family, but because of my actions, I destroyed the gift of life that lost its struggle to live. I retreated to my room, buried myself beneath the covers, and lost myself in regret and sadness. How did this happen? When did I get pregnant?

Yes, Everett and I had major problems in our relationship, but when it came to sex, he and I knew how to stimulate each other. That's why I found it difficult to understand his serial infidelity. Then I remembered the evening he and I walked around the neighborhood. Afterward, we sat on the patio and smoked some marijuana. As I sat back and inhaled, I looked at Everett with intense melancholy. All I needed was his love, and I badly wanted him to make love to me. He saw the depth of my unhappiness, took me in his arms, and held me close. As we embraced beneath the canopy, Everett and I made passionate love. That had to be the night I had become pregnant.

～

Everett stayed close and tried to care for me, but his presence revolted me. I blamed him for my miscarriage. If he truly valued our relationship, I wouldn't have behaved so carelessly. I felt obsolete, and the concept of love was alien. Why me? Why now? Yes, I did things others might consider undignified and dangerous, but that didn't make me a bad person. I knew I had to eventually get out of bed and move forward. I lost a child, but I was still alive.

I was consciously aware of my actions and realized I had to accept the consequences, good or bad. I dictated and set the rules. I took on the characteristics of a man. I had become a man, and I thought and acted like a man. Through my actions, I wanted to hurt Everett as much as he hurt me. I figured if he discovered I was unfaithful, he would get jealous, feel my agony, and change.

Everett knocked on the bedroom door and asked me to meet him outside on the patio. I wanted to ignore him at first, but then I reluctantly went outside and sat in a chair across from him. Initially, we sat there in uncomfortable silence, but then he started to cry. I was astonished. What the hell did he have to cry about? I wasn't in the mood for his bullshit. I had a miscarriage. If anyone should be crying, it should be me.

When he finally stopped crying, he looked at me with bloodshot eyes. "Michelle, I know I've caused you so much pain, but I have to be completely honest with you."

I eyed him suspiciously. "Okay."

"We agreed to always be open and honest with each

other. I know I've failed you, but at this stage in my life, I can't keep living a lie."

"Go on."

"I'm certain you read the text messages on my phone, and I don't blame you. Everything wrong in our relationship is because of me. For most of my life, I've pretended to be someone I wasn't because being accepted by my family was the most important thing to me. To be my authentic self would have been an embarrassment, so I hid in the arms of women. The man sitting here before you is …"

"Well, what?" I said, swallowing my impatience.

"When you looked through my phone, I know you thought I was involved with a few women. Well, that's not the case. I was texting other women." He looked down at the patio deck. "But I was only intimate with one person, and that person was … a man. I just didn't want you to find out about him."

Anger flared deeply within me. "Everett, you're full of shit!" I cried. "There's no way in hell I'm believing you! Dammit, stop lying. Just tell me the truth for once!"

"Will you please listen to me? I'm not lying! I've known for years, but I suppressed my emotions because I had too much to lose. In all my relationships with women, I tried to give my partner the best of me. For me, failure was like a ringing alarm clock I couldn't shut off. I became unhappy and angry and hid my true emotions from my partners. I was fully aware of my actions, and I self-sabotaged the relationships. I just wanted that person out of my life."

I shook my head with a weariness that drained my soul. "Look, Everett, if you want to leave, then leave. I'm not forcing you to stay with me. I'm having a hard time believing you. Did you forget that I caught you with another woman? Or was she a man?"

He looked at me. "She was a woman. When you left on one of your business trips, I went to a swinger's club."

"What?"

"A swinger's club. You know, a place where ..."

"I know damn well what a swinger's club is, so you don't need to explain!" I snapped. I didn't want to cry in front of him, but I could barely blink back the tears.

"Initially, I just walked around and watched," Everett quietly said. "Then this woman, the one we dropped off at the beauty shop, approached me and asked if I planned on participating. I told her more than likely, but not right now, so we talked for a while. Then a man approached, kissed her, and led her away. Before they left, she turned and asked me to join them. I wanted to decline, but I couldn't resist the energy I felt from the man, so I ..."

"What! What did you do, Everett?"

With his head in his hands, he confessed, "I followed them to a private room."

"And?"

"We had a threesome."

"So, what's his name, Everett?"

"Phoenix, and I've been with him off and on for a couple of years."

I leaped from my seat and screamed, "Phoenix! You fucking asshole, you told me there was no Phoenix! Don't you remember, or did you forget? You told me the fucking whore just said that to hurt you!"

I had to stop and take a few deep breaths. I transformed into a bull, and all I saw was red. I thought I'd already been through the worst, but there was still more.

"This ... this can't be happening," I murmured. "Why didn't you tell me? Why did you have to fuck with my emotions? You know I've been struggling with depression, and you did absolutely nothing to help me. I had to fight for my life! And now, you want me to be understanding?"

"Michelle …"

"Don't Michelle me! Now you want to be honest. I was so in love with you and only wanted you to be the man in my life. I gave myself completely to you without hesitation, but what did you do? You trampled my heart and played me for a fool! You made me feel loved, unloved, melancholy, blissful, close, and distant in this relationship! There was nothing I wouldn't have done for you. I knew I should have left your ass, but like an idiot, I stayed. I stayed because I hoped and prayed that you'd change, and I didn't want yet another failed relationship."

"Michelle, I'm so sorry …"

"Really? Well, it's far too late to be sorry. If it weren't for you, I wouldn't have had …"

"Had what?" he asked.

"Nothing!" I snapped. "I can't think right now! You just told me you're in a relationship with a man. How the hell do you expect me to process that? In our relationship, I've always had to compete with a woman, but how the hell do I compete with a man? It's not going to happen!"

"Michelle! Please listen to me. Please!"

With a cloud of hatred hovering over me, I knocked over the chair and stormed into the house. I went directly to my room, slammed the door, and locked it.

Chapter Twenty-Four

I sat in a confused state. Everett's confession felt like a vicious kick to my stomach. For a moment, I couldn't breathe. This couldn't be the life story we painted. It had to be a nightmare that I'd surely wake from soon. Please, Lord, don't let this be real! Did he really prefer men over me? As I sat in stunned silence, I recalled the day Everett asked me to go with him to an adult toy store.

The store was located in a less savory part of town, and I was relieved that there was no one else there except for the impressively tattooed cashier who reeked of weed. The shelves were lined with vibrators in various sizes and shapes along with an assortment of items that defied description. Several racks displayed everything from sexy costumes to full-on bondage gear. I wasn't sure what to focus on, especially with the proliferation of surveillance cameras, so I browsed through the outfits.

From the corner of my eye, I noticed Everett inspecting the vibrators, The selection and sizes were mind-boggling, and I wondered how some could even be used. Was there really a market for this? While I always considered myself adventurous, I felt out of place in this environment.

I approached Everett. "I hope you're not thinking of buying one for me?"

"No, just looking," he said, watching me from the mirrored wall behind the display.

I pasted on a smile. "Is there something you want to tell me?"

"No, like I said, just looking for now, but I need you to have an open mind. Can you do that?"

I hesitated. "Whatever, Everett, sure."

When it came to our sex life, I always trusted him. I knew he wouldn't take things too far or make me uncomfortable, so I walked away and browsed the rest of the store. I was in the shoe section when Everett appeared.

"Ready to check out?"

"Yes," I exhaled with considerable relief.

As we walked to the cashier, I noticed he carried a few items, but quite frankly, I just wanted to get out of the store. I waited by the door while he paid.

When we got home, Everett prepared two drinks, retrieved the marijuana from the kitchen drawer, and motioned me to follow him outside. I remember the evening so vividly. The air was unusually calm, and the skies were painted with vivid rainbow colors. I felt so serene and peaceful that a chill coursed through my body. I thought how wonderful it would be to feel like this all the time.

While I pondered the ethereal skies, Everett reached over and touched my hands. The contact felt like an electrical shock, and the serenity I enjoyed transformed into unease. Why was I so anxious? I'd never felt this way with him before. I needed to calm myself.

"Everett, can you pass me the joint?"

After a couple of hits, I started to relax and enjoyed the

evening. We sat outside for about thirty minutes, sipped on our drinks, and smoked a little more. Everett leaned over and kissed me while his hands gently explored my body. That and the marijuana stimulated every cell in my body and fueled the wetness gushing between my legs.

I moaned. "Everett, if you don't stop, I'm going to explode again."

"Babe, don't hold back. I want your sweet fragrance on me. Let's go inside and take a shower."

After we showered, we went to the bedroom. The bag from the adult store sat on the bed. Everett took out a red, crotchless baby doll outfit that exposed my breasts and handed it to me. "Babe, I got this for you. Please put this on."

While I put it on, he slipped on his robe and left the room. When he returned, he dimmed the lights and said, "Michelle, I want this evening to be special and different."

"Sure, love, whatever you want."

"I'm going to put on some music. I'd like you to dance for me." Then he said, "Zippy, play Marvin Gaye classic hits," and sat on the loveseat while I danced.

Every movement of my round, firm hips against him, along with my heady fragrance, quickened his breath. He gently pulled me onto his crotch, cupped my breasts, and our bodies moved to the rhythm of the music. While it played, he led me to the bed and slowly undressed me, leaving only my heels. Relaxed from the marijuana, I felt I was in a safe space with him. As I stood before him, I wondered what was next. Everett's odd expression was one I'd never seen. It was pleading, almost as if he was asking for acceptance. He then removed a vibrator from his robe pocket.

I stared at it in shock. I wasn't at the register with him when he paid for the items, so I never saw it.

"Everett, what the hell is that?"

"It's an anal vibrator."

"You know I don't feel comfortable using sex toys."

"Michelle, it's for me."

What did I just hear? I stared at him for a few moments. "How … how do I use that?"

"Easy. I'll guide you."

Before using the vibrator, Everett passionately made love to me as if it was our first time, except he didn't have an orgasm, which was unusual for him. Afterward, with a slight tremble in his voice, he asked me to get out of bed. I got up and stood awkwardly. He rose, bent over the bed, and motioned me behind him. He handed me the vibrator and told me to insert it into his ass. Just the thought of doing it made me want to vomit.

I was naive and thought, You want me to put this where? I didn't want to embarrass him. I was already feeling awkward, so I queasily slid the toy into his ass. At this point, I was completely turned off. After I inserted it, Everett asked me to grab his dick. I just put a vibrator in your ass, and now you want me to grab your dick. I reluctantly reached around him with one hand while I tried to grip the vibrator. Suddenly, he began gyrating, breathing hard, and pushed me up against the wall. I didn't have the strength to stop him, so I had to wait for him to climax. He groaned and jerked hard against me several times.

When Everett finally pulled away from me, he removed the vibrator and went to the bathroom. I was shaken and disturbed by what had just occurred and burrowed under the covers. When Everett returned to bed, he tried to cuddle me, but I felt uncomfortable and couldn't relax. He finally turned over and went to sleep.

My thoughts were in chaos. Our sex life wasn't boring. We rarely had sex in bed as we enjoyed the thrill of having sex in the car, on the patio, at a friend's house without their knowledge, and in many other places. So why now? Was Everett gay or bisexual? I couldn't process the thought of him being either, but neither could I ignore how powerfully and quickly he climaxed. It was something he'd clearly experienced before. Perhaps many times.

Disturbed and confused, I pushed the thought to the deep recesses of my mind. I should have accepted then that there was more to what happened than a secret kink. Here I was with a man who had just confessed to having an affair with a man!

As I sat in bed, anger replaced my confusion. Why hadn't Everett been honest with me? What was this double life he was hiding? My heart was shattered by the one person I thought would never let me down. Overcome by rage, I knew it was time to stop being a victim. I had to take action and take it now. I swallowed my rage, got out of bed, and retrieved a small black safe from the top shelf of the closet. I opened it, removed my Smith and Wesson revolver, and loaded it with six bullets.

I stood with the gun in hand. Suddenly, I heard a deafening shattering of mirrors. I jumped and gasped at the jagged shards covering the floor. Bowing my head, I sobbed into my hands. How can this be? Where did these mirrors come from? Is this my life I see on the floor? Sad, shattered, inadequate, destroyed, pathetic, defeated, and on the verge of murder? I knelt, picked up a small shard, gripped it tightly, and watched the blood drip to the floor.

Everett caused this pain. He shattered my heart and caused my miscarriage. Now, he'll bleed as I did. I didn't give a damn. All I wanted was to see his blood and his life drain away. Even if I spent the rest of my life in jail, it would be worth it!

I turned around with blood on my hand, opened the door, and blindly walked down the hallway.

I opened the patio door, walked outside, pointed the gun, and cocked it. Everett's eyes flew open. He raised his hands.

～

He screamed, "No, Michelle! Don't do this!"

"Don't do what? Don't kill you?" As I waved the gun from side to side, I sneered, "You've already killed the love in my heart. You already murdered the life growing inside me. You don't deserve to live! You're a monster! You deserve to die."

Everett reached toward me. "Michelle! Think about what you're doing! Do you really want to spend the rest of your life in jail?"

I laughed coldly. "What the fuck are you talking about? I'm already in jail."

I didn't care what happened to me anymore. I was numb. Empty. Hopeless. I pulled the trigger. The gun recoiled in my hand. I barely heard Everett's scream above the din of the shot and the ringing in my ears. The gun dropped from my hand. I stared dispassionately at the blood pooling from his chest before I turned and walked into the house.

With a gasp, I sat bolt upright in bed. Covered in sweat, my heart pounding, I glanced at Everett asleep beside me. He must have used his key to unlock the bedroom door. Thank God! He was alive. It was only a nightmare! Shaking, I got out of bed and rushed to the bathroom. I splashed cold water on my face and stared at my sad, pitiful face in the mirror. Is this what your life has come to, Michelle? Now you're thinking of murder. This is your solution to the anguish someone else has caused you.

~

The next morning, as painful as it was, I had to be honest and accept my part in our troubled relationship. Everett trusted me, and I felt I should hear him out because we were both responsible.

"Are you okay?" he asked when he found me outside on the patio.

"Hell no, I'm not okay. You caught me off guard. I needed time to process what you told me."

I flinched when he sat down beside me. Noticing my reaction, he moved to another chair.

"I understand." He nodded. "I never felt like I could tell anyone how I truly felt, especially not my family. With you, I felt safe but ashamed. I tried several times to tell you, but I was too afraid. This relationship has been as draining for me as it has been for you. I just can't go on living a lie. I want you in my life, but I want the freedom to be my authentic self."

"Everett, I don't think I can give you what you want. I do love you, but..."

"Can you at least think about it?"

"No!" I stared at him. "You have to understand. It's just too much!"

"Please, Michelle, I need you. You're the only person that truly sees me."

"I have to disagree, Everett. Being with you has been a whirlwind of hopelessness, and the stress caused me to have a miscarriage. I know I should have trusted you and told you, but at that stage in our relationship, we were traveling in different directions."

"Why didn't you tell me? I'm so sorry! I should have been there for you."

"I blamed you for the gift of life that I lost," I said. "If you simply told me that you were bisexual or gay, we could have prevented this tragedy and separated."

"I know I should have been honest with you, but I can't seem to stop myself from repeating the same pattern of self-destruction in my relationships."

I searched his eyes, hoping to find the truth I sought. "Everett, I've always loved and wanted you. Now that you've opened up to me, I also have to tell you something. I'm tired of silence and lies. When you became distant and focused on other women, I did the same. I found comfort in the arms of other men."

"You did what?" he cried.

"You heard me! I was fucking other men and came home and fucked you! That's what!"

Everett's eyes hardened, and his energy shifted to that familiar dark place.

"Well," he sneered, "it's clear you never loved me! If you did, you never would have slept with other men."

I bolted up from my chair and glared at him. "How dare you! How dare you shove your double standard bullshit down my throat when you've not only slept with other women but also a man! So let me get this straight. It's okay for you to suck dick, but I can't. Maybe you can explain the logic here because I sure as hell can't figure it out!"

"Did you forget when I told you that if you wanted to sleep with someone else, we couldn't stay together?" Everett snapped. "Did you at least use protection?"

"It hardly matters now," I retorted, "since I'm not sleeping with anyone! And don't even try to put the mess you created on me! You were the one tomcatting with men and women. Honestly, I should have left your ass, but like a stupid woman in love, I forgave you again and again. But let's not talk about love. If you loved me, your ass wouldn't have been scouring the streets for trash!"

"Michelle, I gave you everything, but you couldn't keep your legs closed."

I laughed sarcastically. "You gave me everything? Well, you must have selective memory. Did you forget that you moved into my home? Yes, I did the same for you, but that didn't stop you from unzipping your pants every opportunity you could! And now you have the audacity to get angry because another man was up in this pussy? I guess you thought I was incapable of attracting another man. Now you feel the pain and despair I've suffered over the past five years. Why the hell are we even arguing? This relationship is over!"

Everett stared at me for a few moments. "You're right, Michelle. There's no point in arguing. But I need you in my life. Please forgive me. There's no one else I can talk to that understands."

At that moment, something in my heart felt like blinds dropping behind a window. "Everett, you need professional help, and I'm not the one. You've lived this lie for years. You can't let shame prevent you from seeking help. I've suffered, and I'm scarred by this relationship. I desperately need healing, but it's impossible if I try to help you."

"Can we at least try?" he pleaded. "Let's just take it a day at a time and see how the relationship unfolds."

I sighed, remembering my mother crying in her room, alone in her suffering. This wasn't how I wanted to envision my future.

"Hell no! Now get out of my house!"

Chapter Twenty-Five

Two months later, alone in my home, I stared at Everett's moving boxes stacked against the walls. I couldn't deny the deep sadness in my heart. All that remained were the movers to collect his personal belongings. After six and half years, the relationship that I had fought to maintain was over. Once again, I was left with only the memories of the man I unconditionally loved — unconditionally loved because I repeatedly forgave him. Trapped in my beautiful home, I felt empty and alone because this was not the life I had planned. While I excelled in other areas of my life, my personal life was a series of disappointments and heartbreaks. I'd transformed into a woman who compromised her values and exhibited the characteristics of a deceptive man.

My thoughts shifted to Chase. If I had stayed with him, just maybe I would have had the life I desired. All he wanted was to postpone the marriage and concentrate on growing his trucking business to provide a comfortable life for us both, but I lost my fucking mind and ended the relationship because I was not getting what I wanted. To silence the painful thoughts in my head, I sat on the patio with a glass of wine and a joint and gazed at the infinite veil of stars. Gradually, I allowed my mind and heart the freedom to acknowledge my mistakes. It was difficult because I wanted to blame Everett for his dishonesty, but I couldn't because he repeatedly revealed his deception and infidelity.

Incidents endlessly replayed in my mind — sleeping with another woman before I became his girlfriend, the woman I caught him with after I became his girlfriend, the way he gazed at the waiters in the restaurant, when he rushed to catch the woman before she fell, when he laughed at the drink thrown in my face, texting with multiple women, and his relationship with a man. No matter how painful Everett's behavior was, there were numerous red flags that I consciously chose to ignore.

My agonizing questions were why I stayed when I constantly rode on an emotional rollercoaster with him. Why did I subject myself to highs and lows of happiness, joylessness, laughter, sadness, gratification, disappointment, pleasure, and grief? The answer was always the same. I wanted us, and I hoped he'd change and recognize that I was the woman who took care of him when he was sick, the woman who listened to his endless work stories, the woman who comforted his distressed spirit, the woman who cooked, cleaned, and never said no to sex.

In our relationship, I lost myself and sacrificed my mental and physical health. I had many opportunities to leave or make a change, but I didn't. I simply stayed and endured. I remained because Everett was affectionate and cared for me as no other man had. He knew how to connect to my spirit and make love to me in ways that transformed me. But he was also a master of hooking me with manipulation and reeling me back into a world of imagined bliss. What was truly fucked up was that I consciously knew what he was doing, but love was so powerful that it distorted my reality.

For years, I hid my personal life in the closet with many broken mirrors. I sacrificed relationships with my family and friends and led them to believe that Everett and I were a model couple. I failed to realize that the ones closest to me could see through my mirrors of deception. I pushed them away with no phone calls, lies, and excuses. I shielded the truth because I feared judgment.

As I gazed in the mirror at my siblings' relationships, I wished for what they had—joy and unconditional love, as well as my parents' approval of their life choices. It was critical to me that I excelled in all aspects of my life. I didn't want to be the child who bore the stigma of failure when my parents anticipated brilliance. With all of my shattered mirrors, I was so consumed with my relation-ships' failures that I didn't notice I was just standing on the doorsteps of my siblings' relationship. I didn't get a clear picture of what truly happened behind their closed doors, so I went into hiding. It may have appeared unrealistic to hide, but it wasn't. It was actually fairly simple because I was embarrassed by the lies, I was living. I could have made the right choice at any time, but I didn't.

I made the purposeful decision to close the door on my family and best friend, Jennifer. I chose, like the women on my block, to suffer in silence and not visit or communicate with them. I opted to suffer the mental abuse in the soli-tude of my bedroom because I believed I was safe with the mirror, and that only the mirror could see me. Like my mother, I thought the bedroom was my safe haven when

Everett was gone. Like my mother, I cried softly and sought solace in the peace of the day. I should have looked in the mirror, seen my strength, and reminded myself that I had to survive for me, just like my mother survived for her children.

~

To move forward, I had to find forgiveness. To forgive Everett, but more importantly, to forgive myself for my destructive behavior and past failures. It took months for me to forgive him, and strange as it may have seemed, we established an honest, lasting, and distant friendship. Our love was like a tornado, turbulent, overwhelming, destructive that destroyed everything in its path. Like Sybil, Everett had many personalities. I saw the little boy who wanted to be held and the man who wanted to be accepted without judgment.

We were both unfaithful and fully conscious of our choices. To find forgiveness for my actions, I accepted and acknowledged the precious moments I would always cherish. The late-night kitchen dances, watching him cook our meals, Everett opening the car door for me, and his gentle kisses, our dinner dates, the amazing sex, and the many times he caught me before I fell. To foster a healthier life and future possibilities, I took time to focus on myself and figure out what I truly wanted out of life. My primary goal was to reconnect with the woman that repeatedly stood in front of the mirror.

I thought I was emotionally equipped to act like a man, but I failed to realize I had careened down a path of destruction. The miscarriage was extremely devastating, and I accepted that my actions damaged my body and may have prevented me from having children in the future. Accepting this loss was difficult, but I hoped the Creator would one day bless me with a family. I acknowledged and accepted that I let the pain from my relationship push me into the arms of other men, men who only offered temporary sexual gratification.

These men infused my spirit with their stains and the stains of their various sex partners. They negatively impacted my mind, body, and soul. I could have changed my behavior, but I was determined to prove a point and was willing to do whatever was necessary regardless of the damage. While I attempted to prove my point, I lost touch with reality and was propelled into a world of lies, deception, and heartbreak. I lived in a hypothetical world that excluded the present. The successful relationship I desperately wanted endured extreme highs and lows. Had I faced the truth and invested the time and energy to address our issues, the happiness I sought could have been within reach.

For years, I did exactly what I wanted. Now, I was reaping the results of my actions. I didn't dwell on the negatives in my life, I accepted the results and my daily walks with loneliness. My change of life occurred when I stopped putting my energy into men. My strength came from my beliefs, and I knew the source of my strength. It was only by the grace of the Creator that I changed directions and survived. I survived without a happy ending, as happy endings are few and far between.

Mirror, Mirror on the wall, this is my final call. I sit with you, reflecting on my life. I now see the strength within me. I compromised my values and did things for him to see. I became an object of imperfection, pretending life's many colors were as radiant as can be. Over and over as I glanced at you, I hid beneath the shadows of reality and disregarded the authenticity of self.

My mirror's perception was fragile but I was aware of my actions. I found fulfillment in the temporary pleasure of sexuality that flowed from the estuary to the ocean that attempted to shatter my existence. I sacrificed years of happiness for overwhelming disappointments that strove to destroy my confidence. Despite knowledge of the mirror's truth, I knowingly chose a path that appeared irreversible. But I now know it's reversible.

Mirror, there's no longer a need for you to catch me before I fall, for I have eagle's wings that soar from the depth of the sea to the highest mountain top. Like a cheetah, I sprint with lightning speed to conquer prey that seeks to devour my soul. I stand like a lioness, protecting my domain of possibilities. Mirror, Mirror on the wall, I'm free! Not shattered, not broken! I stand tall but not alone. Mirror, I finally see me.

Life can mirror a merry-go-round. When you continue to travel in circles, and the scenery never changes, perhaps it's time to get off of the merry-go-round and start exploring a new path of possibilities. To deliberately stay in a toxic relationship can cause mental health issues like despair, low self-esteem, unhappiness, and resentment. When you examine your life and find that things haven't improved, you must look in the mirror, see yourself, and not blame others.

Only when you look in the mirror and admit your mistakes can you discover the insight and strength to move forward. That strength comes from altering your perspective and understanding that if you don't like the reflection you see in the mirror, it's up to you to change it. Change is constant in our life. It can be uncomfortable or rewarding. This process includes accepting the truth about your circumstances and letting go of people and relationships that aren't beneficial.

You must take that initial step; no matter how challenging or seemingly impossible it may seem, you must try. Even if you fail, there's still a tomorrow to try again and improve upon your life. The human mind is a potent instrument. It's a map that can lead you to the pinnacles of glory or the depths of sorrow. You have the power to control your mind. The words you speak can become your new truth. Figure out how to harness this power. Figure out how to master it rather than letting it rule your life.

In your journey of self-discovery, finding what you seek and having the courage to face any unfavorable difficulties head-on can bring about change. Michelle was able to do it, and so can you. You get to design your own life, but sometimes, the plans must be redesigned. There is no such thing as a flawless person, so stop letting others critique your every move. Even if you feel hopeless and your faith has diminished, you should never relinquish your hopes and ambitions for happiness. Don't give up even if someone tries to deter you from pursuing your dreams. Power is in the words that proceed out of your mouth. It's important to pause, take a few deep breaths, and think about how much you're willing to undergo until you finally realize you're wiser and more deserving of a better life.

Life is what you make it. Ernest Holmes said that life is a mirror that reflects to a thinker what he thinks of it. Everything in your life appears in your reflection. Ultimately, if you want to change what you see in the mirror, you must change yourself.